Garnet Wolseley

An English View of the Civil War

Garnet Wolseley

An English View of the Civil War

ISBN/EAN: 9783337223304

Printed in Europe, USA, Canada, Australia, Japan

Cover: Foto ©ninafisch / pixelio.de

More available books at **www.hansebooks.com**

AN ENGLISH VIEW OF THE CIVIL WAR.

II.

BY GENERAL VISCOUNT WOLSELEY, K. P., ADJUTANT-GENERAL OF
THE BRITISH ARMY.

THE second volume of the "Battles and Leaders" is, in my judgment, even more interesting than the first volume. It introduces us to the period when General McClellan transformed the armed masses which had fought at the first battle of Bull Run, together with the vast numbers of recruits who subsequently joined them, into the Army of the Potomac. It takes us through the Peninsular Campaign and dwells upon the deeply-interesting questions involved in its conduct, as well as in its conception as illustrated by later events. It tells us of those two brilliant champions of a lost cause whose leadership is full of military suggestion and military lessons. No matter how doubtful at every point and for all time may have been the legality or advisability of the War, that two such men had fought on any one side would, of itself, throw a halo round the cause they fought for. Their character can never fail to excite general admiration. Even those who were most bitterly opposed to Stonewall Jackson and to Robert Lee, even those who believed them to be utterly wrong in their conception of national duty, will readily admit their excellence as soldiers, their sincerity as patriots.

There is so much to be said on the campaigns in the Shenandoah Valley, on the seven days' fighting near Richmond, on the campaign against Pope, and on Lee's invasion of Maryland, that I must pass over somewhat lightly the most important operations of Admiral Farragut, which led to the capture of New Orleans. Nevertheless, for us of the old country these "amphibious' operations, as Mr. Kinglake would call them, have a quite peculiar importance. The coöperation of the United States navy with their army, in producing a decisive effect upon the whole character of the military operations, is akin to what happens with us in nearly every war in which we engage. A German, a French, or a Russian general may frequently, perhaps usually, carry on a campaign without considering what assistance he may expect to derive from the coöperation of his own navy, or what impediments he may expect to encounter from the operations of the naval forces of his enemy. An English general has almost always to make his calculations strictly in accordance with what the navy can do for him. The operations by which the Federal navy, in conjunction with the army, split the Confederacy in two and severed the East from the West, must always, therefore, have for him a profound interest and importance. The great strategical results obtained by this concentration of military and naval power, which were as remarkable as the circumstances under which the successes were gained, deserve our closest study.

I shall not attempt to discuss from a naval point of view the much-debated question whether Admiral Porter's mortar-schooners were or were not largely instrumental in determining the success of Farragut's passage between Fort Jackson and Fort St. Philip. The point is, however, one in which the effect on the forts is as much involved as the action of the navy. I may, therefore, venture the opinion, based on the evidence of the Confederate side, that the bombardment, considering the enormous number of large shells actually exploded within Fort Jackson, had comparatively little effect in preventing that fort from contributing its share toward the result of the operation. Captain Robertson's evidence (p. 100, Vol. II.) is distinct that at the time of Admiral Farragut's passage, in the water-battery at least, "every gun in the battery was loaded and pointed toward the river, and the men were kept at their posts"; and again: "No guns were silenced in either Fort Jackson or the water-battery at any time during this engagement. Not a man was driven from his post at the guns in the water-battery, much less from the battery itself."

It is, *mutatis mutandis*, almost the same story that General Sheridan tells of the effect of the Prussian artillery at Gravelotte. There the Prussian officers believed they had absolutely silenced the French artillery and crushed out the resistance of the French infantry. From his experience during the Civil War, General Sheridan told them that when they made their attack they would find out their mistake. One of the most bloody repulses sustained by the Germans throughout the war soon afterwards verified the correctness of his inference.

Had it been necessary to silence by mortar fire the guns of Fort Jackson and the water-battery before the ships ran the gauntlet between Fort Jackson and Fort St. Philip, Farragut would never have achieved his splendid success. No! as always in war, Farragut's success was almost purely the result of the moral effect which his movement produced, and of defects other than material in the force opposed to him. It is clear that there was a complete want of unity of command over the combined naval and military defences for the protection of New Orleans. No doubt the Southern fleet was not properly ready for action, and for this unreadiness it would seem that Captain Mitchell, who commanded it, was not responsible. I do not think, however, it is possible to read the correspondence which passed between Captain Mitchell and General Duncan without feeling that Captain Mitchell was one of those men, common enough in every service, who cannot bring themselves to imagine that any one outside their own particular calling is other than a stupid fool. Such men usually conceive it to be their first duty to ignore, as an impertinent interference, any suggestion which comes from outside their own charmed circle. It is clear that the officers in the forts were in a position to observe the movements and to forecast the intentions of the Federals, and that the officers in the ships were not. As it turned out, the "Louisiana" proved absolutely useless to the defence. General Duncan saw through the intentions of Admiral Farragut, but his correct anticipation that the attempt would be made the night it was actually made was an absurd landsman's guess about matters he was not calculated to express any useful opinion upon. His views were, therefore, contemptuously ignored.

Had Captain Mitchell been a man large-minded enough to rise above paltry professional prejudices, he would not have continued to expend all his energies on preparing the "Louisiana" for a service she was never called upon to perform. But he would, on the other hand, have kept "the river well lit up with fire-rafts," as he was again and again urged to do. The temper shown in this proceeding is one so dangerous that, whenever it appears, it deserves to be castigated by those who review the facts afterwards, whether the lash falls on naval or military shoulders. The same temper, it would seem, crops out in Commodore Mitchell's present defence. "Naval officers," he says, "ought surely to be considered better judges of how the forces and appliances at their command should be managed than army officers." Certainly no one will dispute that statement, but both naval and army officers must be judged by a reasonable examination of the results of their action and of the alternatives open to them. On the question whether certain naval officers properly coöperated with and paid proper attention to the representations of the soldiers, a Naval Court of Inquiry is not likely to be the most impartial of tribunals. It would have been interesting if, in appealing to the final judgment of history, Commodore Mitchell had not relied merely upon a naval verdict, which, as he admits, was given without any reception of the evidence on the other side. It would have been well for him to explain why no fire-ships were sent down the river; why the forts were left to fight in the dark during the actual night of attack. Granting that he is correct in urging that by the evening of the 24th April he would have had his ships ready, it would be interesting to know what service he considered he was rendering the Confederacy by preparations which, it was pointed out to him, could not be completed in time for the attack that others believed would be made on the night it actually occurred. To weigh fairly the evidence and to estimate justly the soundness or unsoundness of the reasons and motives which determined Commodore Mitchell's action at the time, it is not necessary to be either a soldier or a sailor. When that officer alleged that he did not take steps to meet the attack on the night between April 23 and 24, because the "Louisiana" would be ready for service by the evening of the 24th, any man of ordinary common-sense will understand that he disbelieved the evidence supplied to him. The evidence went to show that the attack would be made twenty-four hours before the evening of the 24th. Yet surely those reasons for expecting the attack to be made when it did actually come off were absolutely sound.

Such, I think, will be the verdict of independent naval officers, who examine the facts without prejudice. I would sooner have exposed such a line of conduct on the part of a soldier, because my views upon it would then have been more manifestly impartial. But I feel it is important, in the interest of all naval and military states, that these miserable little professional prejudices should be exposed wherever and whenever they occur, for the encouragement of the large-minded men of both services. To do so frankly at all times will, I think, check one of the most fatal tendencies by which the success of any joint naval and military operations may be imperilled, as, in my opinion, the interests of the Confederacy were seriously injured in this instance. To me it seems clear that Admiral Farragut's splendid achievement was made possible, first, by the inadequate previous preparation of the naval part of the New Orleans defences; secondly, by the want of harmonious working between the Confederate naval and military forces; and, lastly, by his own clear appreciation of the moral effect he would produce by forcing his way past the defences of Fort Jackson and Fort St. Philip and by his appearance before New Orleans. For, after all, the forts were never captured by actual attack. They fell because the Confederate soldiers in Fort Jackson mutinied against the continuance of the defence when New Orleans had been captured. It is a curious fact to note that, at that very time, New Orleans— which, however, could not itself be defended—was surrendering avowedly because those forts had fallen! This brilliant result is a striking instance of the due appreciation by a commander of the effect which daring achievements exert on men's minds, although, as in this case, those daring acts do not actually, directly, or materially make certain the end or the surrender they may have secured. In other words, Admiral Farragut's attack was based on a knowledge of the superior importance in war of moral over material force. One can hardly offer a higher compliment to any naval or military commander.

I pass now to the appointment of General McClellan to the command of the Army of the Potomac, and his subsequent accession, for a time at least, to the general command of the armies of the United States. I entertain the strongest possible belief, which has been confirmed by all the evidence supplied by the *Century* papers, that for the failure of the Peninsular Campaign the Administration at Washington was far more to blame than General McClellan. It is, therefore, only fair that I should turn first to the defence of the Administration which has been attempted by Lieutenant-Colonel R. B. Irwin (p. 435, Vol. II.), and examine it in the light of the evidence supplied elsewhere.

General McClellan was appointed on July 25, 1861, to the command of the army in the department of the Potomac, and on November 1 following "to command the whole army" of the United States. He had to create out of purely raw materials an army of which the part he proposed to employ in the Peninsula alone was 156,000 strong. The more one studies the nature of this force as it manœuvred and fought in the Peninsula, and as, despite all its subsequent disasters, it substantially remained throughout the War, the more marvellous does the ability, as well as the rapidity, with which General McClellan organized it appear to soldiers who understand the magnitude and difficulty of the task he undertook. Throughout his whole army, with few exceptions, this appears to have been the view taken by all, from the most senior general to the youngest recruit. But outside the army this was different, although in newspaper articles he was commonly referred to, with more effusion than sense, as the young American Napoleon. They did not hesitate to puff this untried leader as they would have advertised the talents of some rising dentist. As time wore on without bringing any decisive action, there arose throughout the mass of the people an impatience at the delay of preparation, which became daily more apparent. That most cruel tyrant, the "public," had no means of realizing the difficulties to be overcome. It did not understand what organization meant, but it shared with all peoples the very common article of faith that you have only to gather together hundreds of thousands of men, and to arm them, in order to form an army.

As the months of 1862 went by, the universal feeling was one of impatience and restlessness at what was deemed the waste of time and the useless delay which were taking place. Under that impression, and under the force which this so formed Public Opinion was exerting, the Administration at Washington found itself compelled to act. That is evident enough from the most interesting and striking letters which Colonel Irwin quotes as written by Mr. Lincoln to McClellan. It is clear in all of them that the President felt he was being driven by a power superior to his own, and by one to which McClellan, like himself, must yield. "Once more let us tell you," he writes, "it is indispensable to *you* that you strike a blow ! I am powerless to help this." The Administration was merely giving expression to the decrees of an entirely ignorant public opinion. If all those who wield the pen would only kindly wait until commanders have quite accomplished the mission entrusted to them before they decide that soldiers, "with their guns and drums and fuss and fury," are to pass away and leave the glory to others, it might matter little to the state. But when in the middle of a war they take it upon themselves to drive or to force those whom they influence to decide what the naval or military commander should do, the result will certainly be, as it was in this instance, to protract, perhaps for years, the duration of the war which they, in their self-conceit, imagined they could settle off-hand at once.

If these *Century* articles could be as widely read among us as they have been in America, we might possibly be saved in the future from disasters such as were entailed on us in the Crimea by very similar action. In particular, I should like those articles by Mr. Warren Lee Goss, the "Recollections of a Private," duly studied. For, after all, questions of strategy, of tactics, and of the importance of organization of all kinds turn upon the effect which is ultimately produced on the spirit and well-being and fighting efficiency of the private soldier. Whilst the organs of public opinion and their humble servant, the public Administration, were grumbling at the slow movements which only carried General McClellan's army forward fifty-two miles in sixteen days (Colonel Irwin, p. 437), Private Lee Goss and his companions were learning "in time that marching on paper and the actual march made two very different impressions," and though they could "easily understand and excuse our fireside heroes, who fought their own or our battles at home. over comfortable breakfast-tables, without impediments of any kind to circumscribe their fancied operations," they found out also that it is "much easier to manœuvre and fight large armies around the corner grocery than to fight, march, and manœuvre in wind and rain, in the face of a brave and vigilant enemy."

There are, however, matters beyond the immediate view of the private which must be considered. From the moment when, thanks to those mistakes of Mr. Jefferson Davis of which I spoke in the last article, the Federal navy had asserted its absolute supremacy at sea, it is clear that the shortest and safest, as well as the most decisive, route to Richmond was by a movement based on the James River. To carry this out arrangements for the adequate protection of Washington were essential. But whilst McClellan with the main army marched upon Richmond, it was necessary to protect the force allotted for the defence of Washington from a counter-stroke by Lee or by his lieutenant, Stonewall Jackson. To effect this it was desirable to keep it close to Washington, and thus as far away from Richmond as was possible with due regard to the safety of the former city. In order that the army on the James River, intended for offensive operations, should be made as strong as possible, the force detailed for the protection of Washington should have been as small as was consistent with the accomplishment of its object, and should have had a strictly defensive rôle allotted to it. This concentration of energy on a single aim at a time is such a commonplace of ordinary business life that it is passing strange why it should be so difficult to persuade men who have not had the experience of war that in all military operations it is the one thing most needful. Military history, had it been known to Mr. Lincoln and his ministers, would have taught them that, under the then existing circumstances, the Confederate army could not venture far away from Richmond. That threatened capital was not only the seat of the Confederate government, but it was also the base from which the Confederate armies between Richmond and Washington drew their supplies. Whenever attacked, those armies must have returned to defend it.

I think General McClellan ought not to have left Washington without convincing himself that Mr. Lincoln and the Secretary of War were satisfied with the arrrangements he had made for the defence of the capital. That those arrangements were in themselves adequate is beyond doubt. In omitting to come to this understanding with the President, he evinced, it would seem, a want of knowledge of the working of popular governments in times of great national danger. He thus exposed himself to, or, at least, he gave an excuse for, the very thing which happened— that which ruined his chances in the campaign; namely, the withdrawal from his command of at least 63,000 men. Nor was this mere withdrawal of McDowell's corps, of Blenker's division, and of the 10,000 men of General Wool's command, the only disastrous consequence which was entailed on McClellan by the exaggerated fears of the Government at Washington. Secretary Stanton appears to have been encouraged by this first interference with McClellan's plans to take upon himself the general direction of the whole campaign. It was he who thrust forward the force under McDowell, and so entailed upon McClellan the necessity of placing himself in that false position astride of the Chickahominy which led to all the misfortunes of this campaign. It is scarcely possible to imagine any military arrangements more futile than those which were devised by this civilian Minister of War, Mr. Stanton. His scattering of the Federal forces throughout the Shenandoah Valley gave Jackson the opportunity for carrying out his brilliant campaign in that region. The necessity of maintaining connection with the armies which were to come to his support from the North obliged McClellan so to divide his force that, had General J. E. Johnston's orders been properly carried out, the Federal army ought to have had its left wing annihilated at the battle of Seven Pines, as it actually had its right wing crushed at Gaines's Mill.

As already stated, I think General McClellan should have satisfied Mr. Lincoln as to the steps he had taken for the defence of Washington, because that was a subject on which the President had fairly every right to be satisfied; but I cannot admit that this omission on the General's part was any adequate excuse for the complete upsetting of his whole plan of campaign. Mr. Lincoln, though doubtless one of the greatest men who have ruled the United States, was entirely ignorant of war. Able and wise as he was in all matters of civil government, he failed here most disastrously. By the course he pursued he wrecked an ably-devised plan for the advance upon Richmond of all the available Federal forces by one single line, whilst the troops intended for the defence of Washington were kept as passive as possible. Instead of that plan, a divided command was inaugurated and a disjointed series of movements were ordered, which ended in the transfer of the initiative to Lee. The change ordered by Mr. Lincoln in McClellan's plans gave the Confederates an opportunity for throwing their united forces, at pleasure, upon any part of the scattered Federal army. I cannot admit, as Colonel Irwin appears to expect we should all at once do, that McClellan was wrong in refusing to explain publicly to the Cabinet the details of his proposed scheme. At that time it was notorious that what was said to the Cabinet in Washington leaked out at once into the streets, and was thence conveyed promptly to the Confederate authorities. I know, from what I learned at Richmond in the autumn of 1862, how well Lee was kept informed of everything done or intended by the Northern army.

Let us hear Stonewall Jackson on this subject, and compare his methods and principles of action in each particular with those that were pressed on McClellan by the Washington Administration, or, rather, by their master, public opinion. We have to thank General Imboden for those golden sentences of Jackson's which comprise some of the most essential of all the principles of war:

> "Always mystify, mislead, and surprise the enemy, if possible; and when you strike and overcome him, never let up in the pursuit so long as your men have strength to follow; for an army routed, if hotly pursued, becomes panic-stricken, and can then be destroyed by half their number. The other rule is, never fight against heavy odds, if by any possible manœuvring you can hurl your own force on only a part, and that the weakest part, of your enemy and crush it. Such tactics will win every time, and a small army may thus destroy a large one in detail, and repeated victory will make it invincible."

Compare those principles, and the mode in which Jackson carried them out, with the ideas current at Washington, and you will see that they are direct inversions. The orders which emanated from there may be described thus:

> "Go straight at the enemy at the very point where he expects you, and where he has long been expecting to receive you. Let every one know what you are going to do, so that we may announce it in the public press, and chuckle and crow over your coming victory. Scatter your forces in as many directions as possible, so that the enemy may always be able to bring superior forces against you. Arrange your force so that it is rigidly tied to one particular point, and that the enemy cannot doubt where you will be. Go ahead without preparation, forethought, or care; only let us hear that you are moving, so that the newspapers may brag."

These—I declare I have nothing exaggerated and naught set down in malice—these are the principles and practice which Colonel Irwin has undertaken the task of defending. It is a difficult one. I frankly admit that, when dealing with this fatuous folly, General McClellan did not behave with the meekness of an amiable schoolboy under discipline. I think he was unjust to Mr. Stanton in supposing that he (Mr. Stanton) had any personal hostility to him. Mr. Stanton really believed that the orders he gave were transparently sound and wise, and that any one who differed from him must be wrong. I do not know, however, that, placed in General McClellan's position, most generals could possibly have realized this. In order to understand Mr. Stanton it is necessary to read General Pope's account of his interview with that gentleman, given on page 449. One of my friends assures me that in reading it he literally "laughed till he cried," and never fully understood what the expression meant before doing so. I can quite understand it. Laughter is said to be due to our being impelled by two contradictory feelings at the same time. That certainly is the condition under which one reads those pages. There is scarcely any folly possible in relation to the command of an army which Mr. Stanton does not propose with the gravest face to General McDowell. At the same time, the man is evidently sincere, and convinced that, being a clever politician and holding the position of War Minister, every principle of war—*as he understood war*—which he enunciated must be right, and therefore ought to be obeyed without question. It is difficult to pronounce whether the image that rises before us is that of the ignorant stage charlatan who, because his legs are decked with military boots, thinks himself every inch a soldier, or that of a grave Minister who is charged with the solemn responsibility of a great Nation's destiny and with the lives and fortunes of thousands of his fellow-citizens. Let me put a few of the points together.

If there be one thing more important than another in the command of any army, but more especially of one recently gathered together in a hurry from civil life, it is that officers and men should have confidence in their leader. It is essential that they should know and understand him, and, from their previous experience, should feel sure he is going to lead them to victory. "Therefore," says Mr. Stanton, "I cannot be wrong in withdrawing General Pope from the Army of the Mississippi, where he is known and liked and has been doing very well, to take command of the army of Virginia, where no one knows much more than his name, his previous military operations not having been on a scale to command universal attention."

Promotion of a junior over the heads of men very senior to him in the service is often very wise and necessary; but unless it is done for reasons which are known and appreciated by the army as a whole, such as tend to inspire the army with confidence, it is pretty sure to lead to serious friction. "Therefore," says Mr. Stanton, "let us proceed as follows: There are those three corps, which have been chiefly formed under McClellan and are extremely proud of themselves as forming part of the old Army of the Potomac. They have already begun to acquire a certain spirit of their own; disasters have overtaken them for the moment (in consequence, as they believed, of their having been withdrawn from McClellan and foolishly scattered). Let us, therefore, select an officer from a far-off region, belonging to a force of which the Army of the Potomac has a certain amount of soldierly jealousy. The deeds of that distant hero will certainly not be appreciated at their full value by the followers of McClellan. But never mind; let us put this unknown leader over the heads of the three men now holding high command in that army, each well known to his own corps, and each senior to the man we select to command them." With disadvantages of such a nature against him, it may still be necessary sometimes to put an able junior over his seniors, in order that he should undertake some special task, provided he clearly sees his way to accomplish it, and feels confidence in himself. "Therefore," said Mr. Stanton, "let us select General Pope to undertake a task which he himself regards as a 'forlorn hope.' Despite his imploring remonstrances that he may be sent back to his old army, we will order him to 'submit cheerfully,' which will, of course, inspire him with all the confidence he needs." Surely, surely, so far at least every man who manages a large business concern will follow me in seeing that all these propositions denote an insanity that would be ludicrous, if it were not, in such a matter, so terribly criminal.

Upon General Pope, not a strong commander, was now forced the monstrous scheme of moving forward his already hopelessly-scattered army to "demonstrate" within striking distance of Richmond just at the time when McClellan, deprived of that very force, was about to be reduced to inaction by the battle of Gaines's Mill and the retreat to the James River at this junction. General Pope showed his appreciation of the position by urging the appointment of some one general to command the two armies, who could then combine their action for a common purpose. It was a necessity entailed by the attempts to operate at once with both armies, instead of keeping one of them on the defensive and weakened so as to make the other very strong for rapid, offensive operations along the most telling line for an advance. It is obvious that the retreat of McClellan to the James River did make General Pope's position, to the north of Richmond, exceptionally dangerous. It placed the Confederate army absolutely between the two Federal armies, and greatly increased the distance between them. It is not, however, I think, the fact, as General Pope assumes, that the Confederates were "ready to exchange Richmond for Washington." For Jackson's movement to oppose Pope was not made till Lee was convinced that McClellan's army was not in a condition to carry out any further offensive movement. The wide turning movement of Jackson on Manassas Junction, and the movement northwards of Longstreet's corps, did not take place till McClellan had begun to evacuate the Peninsula.

Whatever mistakes General Pope may have made, it is clear that the disasters of this campaign were due to the order from Washington which required him to maintain an advanced position on the Rappahannock, and which gave him reason to suppose that his communications with Manassas would be guarded by troops independent of his own army, but which were nowhere within reach when they were wanted. For that failure General Halleck was no doubt directly responsible; but the great mistake lay in that action of the Administration, which can hardly be better described than in Mr. Lincoln's words applied later in the War: they "swopped horses whilst they were crossing the stream." They allowed McClellan to go off with his army to the Peninsula whilst he was at least nominally in command of the armies of the United States, and as soon as he was fully committed to the enterprise, they so completely upset all his arrangements as to bring about the condition of things which made it necessary to have with the Government in Washington a "General-in-Chief" of all the National forces. General Halleck was selected for the post—a most unhappy, most unfortunate selection.

I do not much appreciate any part of General Halleck's conduct in the War, either when he was in the West or after he arrived at Washington. He appears to have chiefly distinguished himself in the West by snubbing the two ablest soldiers he had under him, Generals Grant and Sherman. He appears to have chiefly distinguished himself at Washington by first snubbing General McClellan, then by placing Pope in a hopeless position, then, immediately after, by giving a positive assurance that Pope was in no danger, to be followed quickly by a complete loss of heart when that General's army came hurrying back in confusion to the Potomac. Then we find him, when panic-stricken for the safety of Washington, throw all responsibility on McClellan, the man he had previously snubbed. As soon as McClellan's presence had restored confidence and *morale* to Pope's demoralized army, he does his best to prevent McClellan from striking effective blows against the very much weaker and, for the time, necessarily dispersed army of General Lee, and we see him, ignorantly and stupidly, incidentally throwing away the forces which were compelled to surrender at Harper's Ferry. It is not, therefore, from any special sympathy with General Halleck that I am induced to think he was, from the first, placed in a false position. He had to take up and accept for better or worse the fatuous plan devised by Secretary Stanton, against which both McClellan and Pope had equally protested. He had to face immediate emergencies before he could possibly have made himself really acquainted with all the circumstances of the new field of war into which he had been suddenly pitchforked.

Hence my own conviction that for this, as for most of the other misfortunes experienced by the Federal troops, the verdict of history will ultimately hold responsible the Administration at Washington rather than the generals who commanded in the field. And yet it is both striking and interesting to see how much the personal character of Lincoln himself rose superior to his surroundings. His very modesty unfortunately left him, as regards all military operations, too much in the hands of his Secretary for War. But compare Mr. Stanton, with "large eye-glasses," "dishevelled appearance," "presence not imposing," "abrupt manner," "speech short and rather dictatorial," employed in dictating orders which were rank nonsense, with the quiet, modest manner, the simple, natural dignity, the genial humor, the shrewd common-sense, which appear in every story told of President Lincoln. One sees clearly enough that, though General McClellan was probably wrong as to the cause which he assigned for Mr. Stanton's opposition to him, he was right enough in attributing his difficulties to the Secretary for War, and not to the President. Mr. Lincoln was, from a military point of view, clearly mistaken in believing that *the* one way to get at Richmond was by making straight there from Washington. It is impossible, however, if one puts one's self at all in his place, not to see how nobly he faced the difficulties of his position, and how anxiously he endeavored to do his duty to his country.

WOLSELEY.

[TO BE CONTINUED.]

AN ENGLISH VIEW OF THE CIVIL WAR.
IV.
BY GENERAL VISCOUNT WOLSELEY, K. P., ADJUTANT-GENERAL OF THE BRITISH ARMY.

I WISH to remind the reader of these articles on the Civil War that they deal only with the information supplied by *The Century* magazine's history of that struggle. The story there told so graphically is treated from the military student's and the military critic's point of view, and it is earnestly trusted that no one may be offended with anything contained in these articles. Many may differ from the conclusions arrived at, and the views expressed may be often or always mistaken; but they are, at least, the honest opinions of one who has the most sincere admiration for the combatants on both sides, and for the many great soldiers and statesmen who then directed the destinies of the United States of America.

The readers of these *Century* magazine papers owe a debt of gratitude to the editors for the pains with which they have collected the various documents. The references to the parts of other papers on the same subject, and to the official publications of the losses and numbers of combatants on both sides, are very useful. But there is one respect in which I would venture to suggest improvement, if any future edition should afford an opportunity. It seems ungracious, where we have been supplied with such a large and costly number of maps, plans, and pictures, to find fault with this aspect of the series. Unfortunately, however, there is one thing needful for a military reader which has not been adequately provided. The text does not seem to have been carefully read by any editor who is in the habit of following, upon the corresponding maps, the movements described. The consequence is, it frequently happens that names of places are mentioned in the text which do not appear in the maps. It is not too much to say that for all purposes of intelligent military study, if the reader had to depend solely on these maps, there is much in the text which might almost as well be omitted. Even when, after much search, the place named is discovered in some map or other, the map in which it is found is often not that which has been prepared to elucidate that part of the narrative. One does not, consequently, get the place shown in relation to other localities described. From time to time references are given to particular maps, but these references are not sufficiently frequent. The references required to other portions of the text, in support of evidence educed, are good and ample, and it is much to be regretted that similar care has not been taken to guide the reader to the map required to elucidate the text upon all occasions.

The third volume covers a series of the most deeply interesting operations of the war. These are, in the East, Fredericksburg, Chancellorsville, and Gettysburg ; in the West, Perryville, Vicksburg, Port Hudson, Chickamauga, Chattanooga, and Knoxville ; to which I may add, for the purposes of this article, the papers at the end of Volume II. on the Mexican campaign and the battles of Iuka and Corinth. To these battles no reference was made in my article in last month's NORTH AMERICAN REVIEW, because they are closely connected with the general sequence of events in the West, which are recorded in this third volume.

For many reasons the three great battles in the East will be considered first.

General Longstreet has made certain comments upon the whole series of papers on those events, which serve as a convenient basis for a discussion of the interesting questions which rise out of them. He himself had a brilliant share in the victory at Fredericksburg. He was absent from Chancellorsville, but he tells us that on his return to the army, prior to the invasion of Pennsylvania, he propounded certain views and principles to General Lee with regard to the general conduct of future operations. I have already quoted Jackson's views as to what he considered to be the guiding principles of war. It is worth while to compare them with those that are laid before us by General Longstreet.

Neither general would probably wish to have a few sentences, such as are here given, taken to represent his whole mind on so large a subject. Nevertheless, it is always a point of some value to notice what are the aspects of the art and science of war which are most forcibly and most constantly present to the mind of an able soldier, for he is almost sure to insist on them, rather than on others, when he has to decide between the advisability of certain plans and methods.

I must, however, express a feeling, which will, I think, be shared by many of those who fought against Generals Lee and Longstreet, that it is not pleasant to read reports by the surviving general of conversations between the two in which he seems to have treated, not to say reprimanded, his great leader more like a school-boy under instruction than like one of the most brilliant commanders and remarkable men of his own, if not of all, time. Whatever other great qualities as a soldier General Longstreet may possess,—and he certainly does possess some very brilliant qualities,—that of appreciating the military genius of the commander under whom he served cannot be reckoned among them.

Most of us think that one commander has seldom been more thoroughly outgeneralled by another than General Hooker was by Lee at the Battle of Chancellorsville. No one has expressed that view more strongly than have the distinguished soldiers who served under Hooker in that battle. Even those who express the warmest appreciation of the skill which Hooker displayed in the manœuvres which brought the army to Chancellorsville think very strongly that it was the difference between the two commanders which sent the Federal Army in retreat back over the Rappahannock, as the result of that battle.

In that battle at least one Federal corps had been utterly broken up and disorganized, though the Federal Army, much better armed, and with an artillery overwhelmingly powerful, numbered 130,000, and the Confederates only 60,000, men. With such a disproportion of force, that the effect of the battle should have been, not merely to stop the invasion of the South, but to open the way for the Confederate invasion of Pennsylvania, would seem, one would say, to imply that the Federals had been "outgeneralled." Yet, on returning to the army, General Longstreet's only view, not alone of this campaign, but of that in the Shenandoah Valley under Jackson, of the first and second Bull Run, and of the Peninsula campaign, appears to have been expressed by saying that "one mistake of the Confederacy was in pitting force against force. The only hope we had was to outgeneral the Federals." "The time had come (*sic*) when it was imperative that the skill of generals and the strategy and tactics of war should take the place of muscle against muscle."

"We"—that is, Longstreet and Lee—"talked on that line from day to day, and General Lee, accepting it as a good military view, adopted it as the key-note of the campaign." I do not know how it will strike others, but to me there is something unspeakably pathetic about the picture of Lee—that man alike of marvellous modesty and marvellous genius, who by his skill and daring was then exciting the admiration of all that world from which he was cut off—thus closeted with his carping lieutenant. How could Lee do otherwise than accept it as the key-note of his campaign that he must endeavor to compensate for the numerical weakness of his army by the skill of his dispositions? On what else had he to rely than the devotion of his soldiers and their confidence in him? But how cruel a blow to such a man must it have been to discover that, after all their campaigns together, the general who was now left him as the right arm on which he must rely had formed this conclusion as to all his handling of the army in the past! Apart altogether from mere personal feeling, which, seeing that Lee was human, must have been sore enough, how serious a weakness did this disclose in one of the most important elements of his possible strength! Imagine the difference between having to rely for the carrying-out of your plans upon a soldier whose judgment and estimate of you were of this kind, and upon one who had for you the feeling which Jackson showed for Lee when he declared, "That man is a phenomenon. I would follow him blindfold anywhere." Yet it was from the same campaigns that the two great lieutenants of Lee had drawn these opposite conclusions.

We are not, however, left in any doubt as to the nature of the strategy which Longstreet desired to see adopted, or the nature of the experience on which he founded it. He writes :

"I then accepted his proposition to make a campaign into Pennsylvania, provided it should be offensive in strategy, but defensive in tactics, forcing the Federal Army to give us battle when we were in strong position and ready to receive them. . . . I stated to General Lee that, if he would allow me to handle my corps so as to receive the attack of the Federal Army, I would beat it off without calling on him for help except to guard my right and left, and called his attention to the battle of Fredericksburg as an instance of defensive warfare, where we had thrown not more than five thousand troops into the fight, and had beaten off two-thirds of the Federal Army, with great loss to them and slight loss to *my own* troops. I also called his attention to Napoleon's instructions to Marmont at the head of an invading army."

Now, it is certainly not wished to disparage the advantages of this method, where it can be adopted, of offensive strategy and of defensive tactics. Most generals believe distinctly in the possibility and advisability, under certain circumstances, of taking up such a position that by your doing so your enemy will be forced to elect between an attack under very great disadvantages upon your strong position and the abandonment of some most important object. But as the wise man has said of "every purpose under the sun," so it may be said of war, there is a time to attack and a time to refrain from attack, a time to defend and a time to abandon the defensive. Judged by the criticism General Longstreet offers of the action of others, his principle would appear to imply that, when an army has the opportunity of striking a series of blows against isolated fragments of its enemy, it ought to refrain from taking advantage of them in order to adopt the policy he advocates. It is needless to point out how directly that principle brings him into conflict with the admirable views on war of Stonewall Jackson, which were quoted in the article on this subject published in the July REVIEW.

Of the Fredericksburg campaign, apart from the battle, we unfortunately get very little account in these papers. Most students of war will, it is thought, consider the especial brilliancy of that campaign to have depended upon the mode in which Lee succeeded in bringing up Jackson exactly at the right moment. This was done so cleverly that the Federal commander committed himself to the attack on the Confederate Army under the impression that he had little more than Longstreet's corps to deal with. Without that application of Jackson's principle, Longstreet would have intrenched at Fredericksburg in vain. It is not often you can induce your antagonist to attack straight to his front the position you have worked at for weeks to strengthen, and especially where it is a position upon which he can bring no adequate artillery fire to bear. To quote Napoleon as meaning that, when an opportunity presents itself, you ought not to strike with your own concentrated army that of your enemy before it is concentrated; that you ought not, as Jackson did at Chancellorsville, to bring an overpowering force upon the flanks and rear of an exposed wing which can be dealt with before it is supported, will seem absurd to any one who knows what Napoleon did, and why it was he so severely criticised Marmont's proceedings.

Indeed, it is difficult to believe that an able soldier like General Longstreet can really mean this. There is often an indisposition, not uncommon among able men, to play second fiddle, and to be very critical of the first fiddle. It is easiest to account for General Longstreet's proceedings by assuming that he was no stranger to this feeling. In order to enforce the wisdom of the advice he gave his chief, General Longstreet records a forecast that he made in regard to the battle of Sedan. He would appear not to have closely studied the circumstances of that battle, for otherwise he would be aware that, while he was quite right in predicting that "MacMahon's army would be prisoners of war in ten days" from the time at which he spoke, he was entirely wrong as to the method by which that result would be brought about. The Prussians at Sedan did not "force MacMahon to attack," but attacked *him* on all sides. They carried Bazeilles after fierce and bloody attacks. They carried by attack La Moncelle, Daigny, Givonne, the plateaus above Floing and Illy, and the Bois de la Garenne. They only refrained from an actual attack with their infantry upon the immediate neighborhood of Sedan because, having already secured by attack all the positions which commanded the valley, they were able to bring such an overwhelming artillery fire to bear that the French position became untenable.

In no sense whatever is the battle of Sedan an example of offensive strategy and of defensive tactics. The campaign of 1870 and the principles of war followed by the German leaders are most unfortunate authorities for General Longstreet to appeal to in support of his special views. The modern German writers on war seem to enforce a theory the exact opposite to that of General Longstreet, to an exaggeration as extreme on their side as his appears to be on the other. They for the most part seem to admit as little as he does "that there is a time for every purpose under heaven"; there is, however, this one great difference between them: that, whereas he assumes the one great method of war to be that of offensive strategy and defensive tactics, they, most of them at least, continually urge that offensive strategy implies offensive tactics. They are also very strongly impressed with a view which, if we may judge from their conduct of war, appears to have been that of both Stonewall Jackson and of Grant, and perhaps that of Lee also—that defensive tactics carried on behind intrenched positions have a very dangerous tendency to unfit soldiers for all rapid offensive action. That is a serious element in the whole question which must be taken into account. It is completely ignored in General Longstreet's criticism of Lee.

In these remarks, the actions of Fredericksburg and Chancellorsville have been taken together, as the story of those battles seems admirably to illustrate Lee's principles and method, and to clear the way for the discussion of Gettysburg also.

I cannot, however, pass on to the Gettysburg campaign without calling attention to Lee's mistake in allowing the Federal Army to escape across the Rappahannock after the battle of Fredericksburg. To command in war for many campaigns and make no mistakes is impossible. General Lee, great in strategy and able in tactics, is no exception to the wisdom of this saying. Military history can only be made of use to the student of war by a close criticism of every operation, and the critic, no matter how humble, should not shrink from pointing out what he conceives to be the errors and mistakes made by even the most renowned commanders. General Lee made some mistakes in his most brilliant career, but the greatest was after the battle of Fredericksburg. The more closely his conduct then is studied, the more inexplicable it appears. The reasons he gives in his published despatches for having failed either to push the Federal Army into the river or to compel its surrender are most unsatisfactory, most insufficient. (Page 82—note.) When the last Federal attack was repulsed on that eventful 13th December, Burnside's army was at Lee's mercy. It is, however, easy to be wise after the event, and to point out what might or ought to have been done. When Wellington realized that the battle of Waterloo was won, he is proverbially reported to have suddenly shut up the telescope through which he had been looking, and to have given the order, "Up, Guards, and at 'em." He felt that the time had come for passing from the defensive to the active offensive, for he saw that Napoleon's army had been delivered into his hands. Yet that army had no unfordable river, like the Rappahannock, immediately behind it. Had the French army on the evening of the 18th June, 1815, been situated as Burnside's army was on the evening of the 13th December, 1862, none of it could ever have succeeded in recrossing the Belgian frontier into France.

It has always seemed to me that, if Burnside's army had been destroyed, as it ought to have been, after its crushing repulse at

Fredericksburg, the struggle between North and South would have assumed an entirely different aspect, and subsequent events would not have been as they were. That army was by far and in every way the finest under the Federal flag, and was the nucleus of that which afterwards fought at Gettysburg, and which eventually forced General Lee to surrender. The prize in front of the great Confederate general was enormous. He would doubtless have lost very heavily had he left his position of vantage to push the defeated Federals into the Rappahannock, but the losses at Chancellorsville and by many other subsequent battles might have been thereby saved. Lee does not seem to have realized how great was the Federal loss and how serious the demoralization of their army on the evening of the 13th December. He made up his mind that Burnside would renew the fight next morning, and the pages of *The Century* magazine tell us how fairly justified he was in thinking this, as they show that Burnside meant to have done so. Had the Federals attacked again on either the 14th or 15th December, judging from Lee's general mode of fighting, I think we are entitled to assume that he would, without doubt, have followed up a second repulse of the Federal attack by such an immediate and vigorous offensive as would have annihilated Burnside's army. It must be admitted that, whilst Lee's position was admirable for a passive defence, it was very bad for the sudden assumption of an active forward offensive when the enemy's attacks upon it had been even crushingly repulsed.

During the course of this long war some great opportunities were lost by the Confederacy for the delivery of a death-blow to the Northern armies. But upon no other occasion was the opportunity so apparent, or the results that would have attended success so evident, as at Fredericksburg. That battle was a brilliant success. Lee ought to have made it a crushing, if not a final, victory.

Burnside's retreat to the North bank of the Rappahannock during the stormy night of the 15th December was admirably conducted, and most creditable to the Federal generals and staff officers who carried it out.

Every one is agreed that the first day's fight of Gettysburg was brought on without Lee's having expected it. On that day two Federal corps had been severely handled by very superior Confederate forces. The Federal Army was neither concentrated nor were its corps near enough to the battle-field to be concentrated by the time that the Confederate Army ought to have been able to attack them. The evidence adduced as to the position of the Confederate corps is incontrovertible. Colonel Allen, in his reply to General Longstreet (page 355), has shown conclusively, not only that the reports of all the division commanders at the time are directly against General Longstreet's assertion that his divisions were "fifteen or twenty miles away from the battle-field on the night between the 1st and 2d July," but that General Longstreet's own official report at the time contradicts his recent statement on this point. The soldier instinctively admires the fine fighting qualities of General Longstreet, but the student of war called upon to express an opinion upon his conduct, when second in command to General Lee, sees much to find fault with. General Longstreet tells us (page 340) of his somewhat fierce discussion with his chief on the afternoon of the 1st July as to the plans that should be followed in the next day's battle. The account we have already had of his earlier conversations with Lee upon the general conduct of the war throws an interesting light upon what must have passed through Lee's mind during those discussions.

That Lee felt the necessity of keeping on the kindliest terms with his able, but argument-loving, lieutenant is evident. He bore with characteristic humility what must be termed the essentially disrespectful attitude of mind towards him of the man on whom he was obliged to rely for the most important stroke of the whole war. But that all the time Lee's own mind remained clearly fixed on the policy of adopting either offensive or defensive tactics, according to circumstances, is manifest from the firmness with which he rejected Longstreet's proposed plans. He was determined not to lose the opportunity which chance had thrown in his way, for the very doubtful possibility of being able to manœuvre round the Federal army—an operation which would, at least, certainly afford that army time to concentrate against him. By all that is recorded in this volume of General Longstreet, by his whole conduct on the 2nd and 3rd July, and by the tone and temper of his present writings, it seems very evident that he quitted Lee on the night between those two days with his mind filled with the fixed idea of defensive tactics. His thoughts were apparently too much absorbed with his own plans to admit of his paying a properly strict attention to the orders and directions of his chief. Yet upon their prompt and accurate execution depended the success of Lee's far more brilliant and far wiser scheme of action.

General Longstreet has appealed to Napoleon. Those who have most carefully studied Napoleon's methods and habit will think, I believe, that Napoleon in Lee's place would have attacked in the early morning of July 2, as Lee intended to do. Those who have closely followed the history of this war will also be inclined to think that, if Jackson had been in Longstreet's place, the attack would have been delivered before 10 A. M. at the latest.

With the evidence given in this volume before us, few can doubt the truth of Colonel Allan's statement (page 356) that

"General Longstreet, though knowing fully the condition of things on the night of the 1st, knowing that Lee had decided to attack that part of the Federal Army in his front, knowing that every hour strengthened Meade and diminished the chances of Confederate success, and knowing that his corps was to open the battle and deliver the main assault, consumed the time from daylight to nearly 4 P. M., on July 2, in moving his troops about four miles over no serious obstacle and in getting them into battle."

The evidence now laid before us goes far to show that General Longstreet was not only responsible for the fact that his own wing attacked so late that almost the whole Federal Army was concentrated before the stroke was delivered, but also for the fact that he was, when the attack was delivered, not properly supported by the other parts of the army detailed to coöperate in the attack. When the principal attack, on which all others depend, is delivered at least six hours later than it is ordered to be delivered, it is impossible that coöperating corps should time their movements so as to support it. General Longstreet has clinched the evidence as to the cause of the imperfect success of the battle on the second day, by urging that Lee had not ordered the attack to be delivered at the earliest possible hour on the 2d July. The direct evidence brought against him on this point is, however, very clear, although even without such evidence it would still be clear to all who closely study this great battle that the whole point and scheme of Lee's battle manifestly depended on the attack being delivered at the earliest possible moment. If General Longstreet had not been too much absorbed by his own ideas of the way in which the campaign ought to have been fought, to pay attention to the literal and prompt execution of his chief's orders, he must have seen for himself that suddenness and earliness in the attack were of the essence of that scheme.

Similarly, in the third day's battle all the evidence goes to show that, if Pickett's attack had been supported by the whole force of Longstreet's corps and the division and a half of H. P. Hill's corps, which were put at his disposal, that attack would have succeeded. The picture of General Longstreet not even able to make up his mind to order the charge of Pickett's division recalls the bitter memories of our own attack upon the Redan in September, 1855. Upon that occasion our final repulse was due to want of support. No effective arrangements had been made to reënforce the British troops engaged in the assault, who, left without support, were easily disposed of by the fresh troops of the enemy brought to bear on them. No operation in war is so bloody, nothing is so cruel to all concerned, as the weak decision which allows an insufficient force to engage in an attack from a disinclination to expose more than a small number of men to the risks it entails. How many serious disasters have been occasioned by the tender-heartedness of the commander who lacked the moral courage to launch heavy columns in support of men engaged in an attack like that attempted by General Pickett!

As to Lee's decision to attack on the third day of Gettysburg, intending that attack to be adequately supported (as, however it was not), it is very interesting to compare this battle with that of Grant at Chattanooga. Few will contend that the advantages which General Grant had gained during the first two days' fight at Chattanooga were so great as those which Lee had gained in the first two days' fight at Gettysburg. On the first day at Chattanooga, the 23d November, 1863, Thomas's force seized the picket lines of the enemy in front of him by a sudden rush. On the 24th, Hooker, on the right, drove in a small force of the enemy, and secured the evacuation of Lookout Mountain, and Sherman forced his way to a position detached from the enemy's right; but up to the moment when the successful charge was made in the centre by Thomas, General Sherman had entirely failed to force his way on the left, and General Hooker had not made good his advance on the right. No doubt the charge of Thomas, as actually ordered, was not intended to be carried forward in the way it was. But a comparison between the circumstances of Thomas's successful charge at Chattanooga with the eral Longstreet's statements of at least some of their value as evidence, and his criticism of all value as that of an unbiassed judge.

There is in the record of General Longstreet's battles a uniformity of incident as marked as that noticed in the case of some other generals. In the first day's fight at Seven Pines, according to all the best evidence that is before us, General Longstreet's division was so long in getting into position and preparing for attack that the whole scheme of General J. E. Johnston miscarried. General Johnston has too great a respect for his lieutenant, and is too generous a man, to reproach him for the miscarriage. At the second Bull Run, according to General Longstreet's own report (page 519, Vol. II.),

"As soon as the troops were arranged, General Lee expressed a wish to have me attack. The change of position on the part of the Federals, however, involved sufficient delay for a reconnoissance on our part. . . . The position was not inviting, and so I reported to General Lee. . . . General Lee was quite disappointed by my report against immediate attack along the turnpike. . . . General Lee urged me to go in, and, of course, I was anxious to meet his wishes. At the same time I wanted more than anything else to know that my troops had a chance to accomplish what they might undertake."

And so on *ad libitum*—Lee always anxious for attack; Longstreet deliberating and postponing action. In his one brilliant and successful attack during all these battles—that at Chickamauga—Longstreet, being commander of the Confederate left wing, and having orders (page 652, Vol. III.) from Bragg to "begin at daybreak," did not (page 655) "advance until noon," by which time the action of the other wing had caused a gap in the Federal lines through which Longstreet, brilliantly taking advantage of the error, advanced and caused the Federal defeat. "Discovering, with the true instinct of a soldier, that he could do more by turning to the right, he disregarded the order to wheel to the left, and wheeled the other way." Destiny may have shaped these results, but one is much mistaken if there is not evident in each of these actions the hand and mind of the same man who rough-hewed each of them according to the same temperament—the hand of one man who was much better adapted to repair the errors of a second-rate commander than to carry out the purposes of such a chief as Lee. There is a greatness of soul which may be shown in subordinating even a better judgment to the perfect carrying-out of the scheme of a leader who has the right to decide. Of any recognition of that fact on General Longstreet's part in his relations with Lee, no trace is to be found in any one failure of Pickett at Gettysburg will show that a large element of the uncertain prevailed in each case, and that it by no means follows that, because Pickett's charge proved in fact disastrous, Lee was therefore wrong to order it, or that, if it had been properly supported, it would not have succeeded. Even if we had not the direct and specific evidence of General Imboden, we could not doubt that the words he has quoted must have represented the secret thoughts of Lee.

"I never saw troops behave more magnificently than Pickett's division of Virginians did to-day. In that grand charge upon the enemy. And if they had been supported as they were to have been,—but for some reason not yet fully explained to me, were not,—we would have held the position, and the day would have been ours."

After a moment's pause he added in a loud voice, in a tone almost of agony, "Too bad! Too bad! Oh, too bad!" (Page 421.)

The whole story, as told by General Imboden, of that casual meeting with Lee at 1 A. M. the morning after the last day's battle, seems to leave no doubt as to what Lee's view of the facts really was. Nothing is more characteristic of the man than that, when quietly reviewing the situation, he should realize how all-important it was to the cause of the Confederacy that no personal differences should arise between him and Longstreet, and that he should consequently have taken all the blame upon himself. Most soldiers will think that General Longstreet has not served his own cause well by appealing so much to the generous silence of his chief. He has, at least as far as all future histories of the war are concerned, deprived himself of the benefit of that silence by the way in which he has laid himself out to make charges against the chief who refrained, under the most dire provocation, from one word of reproach against him. The sneer about the appointment of Virginians to command has been well answered by Colonel Allen; the sneer about Stuart's "wild ride around the Federal army" (page 355), which General Longstreet asserts was undertaken in disobedience of his own orders, is unfortunate, as Colonel Mosby (page 251) shows from the original document that it was made by General Longstreet's own order, after the question had been expressly referred to him by General Lee : the errors he has fallen into as to the position of his own corps prior to Gettysburg are similarly confuted by the original documents. These, and not a few other matters of similar character, seem to deprive Genof these actions. That Longstreet was a brilliant leader of a division or wing in action there can be no doubt, but he seems never to have been able—perhaps from some peculiarity of temperament—to subordinate his own views heartily to the views and orders of his great chief. The impartial military critic must admit that at Seven Pines, the second Bull Run, and Gettysburg, the Confederacy paid dearly for that defect in his character.

In one respect there is a rather remarkable similarity in the incidents of the Gettysburg and of the Chancellorsville campaign. In the latter campaign nearly the whole of the Federal cavalry had been detached from the army in order to throw itself between Lee's position on the Rappahannock and his base at Richmond. The major portion of the Federal Army then crossed the Rappahannock, and the battle of Chancellorsville was fought whilst the Federal cavalry was thus absent. During the Gettysburg campaign, Stuart, with a large portion of the Confederate cavalry, had been detached round the rear of Meade's army, and the other portion of the cavalry, having been, by the course of the movements, thrown out of the line between the two armies, Lee was left with no cavalry in his front at the moment when the collision between the two armies unexpectedly occurred at Gettysburg. There is just this difference—that during the Gettysburg campaign the absence of the cavalry was contrary to Lee's intention. He had calculated upon its being possible for Stuart to return to him before the collision should take place. The difficulty which a body of men, launched like those of Stuart upon the rear of an army, find themselves in, is well likened to the position of a man turned blindfold in a room full of enemies. It was that difficulty which prevented Stuart's return till the eve of the battle. In the case of the Chancellorsville campaign, Hooker's scheme deliberately involved his being deprived of the services of the cavalry during the course of his whole campaign. In both cases alike the result seems to show that, when armies are manœuvring against one another in the field, it is a risk too great to be worth running, even for the sake of breaking in upon the communications of an enemy, to deprive the army of its eyes, as one must do if the bulk of mounted troops are sent off on some entirely isolated operation.

The case of Stuart's ride around McClellan, during the Peninsula campaign, is altogether different. There the armies were for the time stationary when opposite one another. Lee had no intention of undertaking any movement till his cavalry had returned. Stuart brought back most valuable information, which assisted greatly in the general movements of the subsequent campaign. Similarly, the partisan work of small parties like that of Colonel Mosby may serve a most useful purpose, and cannot be conducted with too much audacity. But Stoneman's raid seems to have gained advantages for the Federal Army which, though important, were dearly purchased by the loss of the battle of Chancellorsville. The more one considers that battle, the more clear it becomes that it was the absence of the Federal cavalry which made possible Jackson's turning movement. Under ordinary circumstances, the detachment of so large a force as that of Jackson's to move at first completely away from the battle-field, and then round the enemy's flank and rear, would be a very risky undertaking. It was possible and successful, first, because from the nature of the country nothing of the movement could be seen from the actual Federal position until it was too late, and, secondly, because the Confederate cavalry were able, in the absence of any corresponding force on the other side, to feel all the approaches to the Federal position and to ascertain exactly where their right wing lay. The small number of possible exits from the Federal position towards that of Lee made it possible for Lee to hold them as if they were defiles, whilst Jackson, with the help of the cavalry, was working round to the vulnerable point.

The whole story of the Federal action during these battles seems to carry the same moral as that which is pressed in my first article. The decisions from Washington and the criticisms from Washington, based upon the loose and rampant public opinion of the day, were in every instance wrong, and were disastrous to the cause of the Union. Well would it be if the survivors of the Administration by which those hasty judgments were formed would now realize what the effect was of their deciding upon the course of action to be taken without having before them any of the data for such decisions. If now they would only understand the danger they entailed upon their country by their interference in the conduct of war—the most difficult of all arts—without any knowledge of its methods or of its principles, one might hope that the chastened and wise public opinion so formed would be an incalculable future benefit to all self-governing nations.

[To Be Continued.]   Wolseley.

AN ENGLISH VIEW OF THE CIVIL WAR.
V.
BY GENERAL VISCOUNT WOLSELEY, K.P., ADJUTANT-GENERAL OF THE BRITISH ARMY.

IN MY last article I dealt with the operations in the East, which are described in the third volume of *The Century's* papers on the Civil War. With a few further remarks on that subject, I shall pass on to consider the story of the campaigns in the West, which are also placed before the public in that volume.

The silence which was necessarily imposed upon General Burnside by loyalty to the Federal authorities has been, fortunately for us, broken through by Major Mason's highly irregular, but very interesting, personal invasion of General Burnside's headquarters. Very dramatic, certainly, is the scene described (page 101) where the Federal commander, after his terrible defeat, sitting "on an old log and being provided with crackers, cheese, sardines, and a bottle of brandy (all luxuries to a Confederate), discussed this lunch, as well as the situation," with the Confederate officer who had surreptitiously secured the interview with him.

It is very characteristic of that kind of West Point comradeship which was never wholly lost among the men who, on the two sides, were doing their best to kill one another, that Burnside should have been anxious to let the able soldiers opposed to him know, what he could not tell his own army, "that he was not responsible for the attack on Fredericksburg in the manner in which it was made, as he was himself under orders and was not much more than a figure-head."

Who, then, was responsible for this and for similiar incidents? There exist in all professions certain men who make their way in the world by pandering to popular prejudices. In the army and the navy the form which this particular quality takes is one which is common in all countries, but in England and America it has a special character of its own. During peace, the business of these men is to find excellent military reasons for the penny-wise economies which suit the taste of ministers who want to present a favorable budget to their countrymen. During war, their business is to clothe in military phraseology, and perhaps in army orders, the current popular prejudices of the time. Now, there is no wish to judge here of General Halleck's private character, or to say that, as a public servant, he may not have possessed many high qualities. But, taking the history of these campaigns from the time when he was appointed to the general command of the armies of the United States till the moment when, on "the coming of Grant," he was reduced to the position of a highly useful subordinate, I cannot trace the least evidence of his having ever given a decision which represented more than the embodied prejudices of the moment. There was a popular feeling that the mighty Army of the Potomac ought to brush from its path and easily destroy its numerically-inferior opponent; therefore the one thing said to be wanted was that it should go straight at its enemy and attack that enemy wherever found. Hence the orders from Washington for the disastrous attack on Fredericksburg, and hence the fatal persistence in that attack after all chance of surprising Lee, or of taking him at a disadvantage, had utterly disappeared.

When Lee began to move to his left after Chancellorsville, he offered General Hooker an obvious opportunity to overwhelm his right, which was still at Fredericksburg, and to threaten Richmond, long before any possible danger could have arisen to Washington with its powerful defences. But Lee was able to count with confidence upon the fears of a capital city and of the government within it for their own safety. The event proved that he was right. The mere suggestion by Hooker that to attack Lee's right was the proper course to pursue was sufficient to cause the removal of that general from his command. After Gettysburg, the popular impression appears to have been that the Confederate Army had been routed and that the Federal Army was virtually intact. The true state of the case was that the Confederate Army had certainly suffered very severely. It had been repulsed and defeated, but it was in no sense disorganized, and the Federal Army was in no condition for an effective general advance.

According to the evidence supplied by this volume, General Meade, at Gettysburg, appears to have done all that any one but a man of quite transcendent military genius could have done to organize an effective pursuit. Few soldiers can, therefore, read without some angry feeling the letter which Halleck then sent to Meade.

> 'I need hardly say to you that the escape of Lee's army without another battle has created great dissatisfaction in the mind of the President, and it will require an active and energetic pursuit on your part to remove the impression that it has not been sufficiently active heretofore."

That feeling must necessarily be increased by his further missive in answer to Meade's natural and immediate reply, asking to be relieved from the command of the army. "My telegram stating the disappointment of the President at the escape of Lee's army was not intended as a censure, but as a stimulus to an active pursuit." Clearly General Halleck was in his wrong place. If, after Meade had won for the Federals the first great victory of the war over Lee's army, it was advisable then and there to remove him, the first letter would have been a fitting preparatory step to that end. Otherwise, to say that it was not a censure, and yet send it, was an act of feebleness, and displayed great ignorance of how a general commanding an army in the field should be dealt with. What pursuit had Halleck carried out after Shiloh? Of all men in the war, Halleck was the last who ought to have reproached another man for not adequately reaping the fruits of victory. Jackson's principle is always sound—never to "let up in pursuit" while pursuit is possible. But pursuit must have been begun in order to be followed up. An attack on the Confederates on the 4th July, if it had been possible for the Federal Army, would probably have been disastrous to the Confederates, because of their want of ammunition. No one who was not then present in the Federal Army can judge if it was possible. No one who was present at Gettysburg seems to have considered that it could be made. Under those circumstances, Halleck's business, as the chief military adviser of the government, was clearly to have pointed out to the President, "It is impossible to judge without being on the spot whether it would have been possible to do more than Meade has done; but as long as we retain him in command we must give him every sign of our confidence and all encouragement." It would have been easy so to word an earnest belief in his future success as to suggest an eager pursuit.

It is not proposed to enter closely into what is called the "Meade-Sickles controversy." There are evidently exaggerations on both sides. General Meade, having only just succeeded to the command of the army before the battle of Gettysburg, was in a very difficult position. He seems to have used considerable judgment in the mode in which he brought up his reserves to the right place and at the right time. If he was unjust, as he is charged with being, in his report of the share of the different corps in the action, he only failed in what is an almost impossible task. No general can know for long after a battle all the details of what has happened in it. On the other hand, "councils of war" are recorded under Meade and other generals in this war as though they were the most natural and legitimate things in the world. It is difficult to conceive the circumstances under which such councils as are here described, and by means of which the general in command would seem to endeavor to transfer his own responsibility to the shoulders of the majority of the council's members, can be other than a blunder and a sign of weakness. Newspaper reports of wars have, I think, often tended to create very unfortunate popular impressions as to the frequency of these councils in all campaigns, which may even affect soldiers. Whenever a number of generals are known to be assembled at headquarters, those in search of news naturally jump to the conclusion that some event is about to take place, and announce to their readers that a "council of war" is being held. Nine times out of ten the generals have only been assembled to give such information as they possess, to state their views, and to receive their orders. The character of such a proceeding is altogether changed when it is announced as a deliberative " council of war"—the abomination of all strong men, a byword for inefficiency and want of decision, and for weakness of action in all military matters. The decision of Meade's " council of war" on the second day at Gettysburg, like that arrived at by most councils of war, was not to attack, and, therefore, as it fortunately proved, to remain where they were and accept battle. This decision cannot be taken as a model for future imitation, though it happened in this instance to be the right course, as it turned out.

On one point more there is a word to be said before we pass from the East to the West. The evidence appears to be clear that on the afternoon of the first day of Gettysburg, at 4 o'clock, General Ewell had his corps, 20,000 strong, ready in column of attack to assault Culp's Hill. (Page 411.) The evidence is equally clear that, in all human probability, if that attack had then been delivered, it would have been successful, and that, if successful, the whole of Cemetery Ridge would have become untenable. Further, it is clear that Lee stopped that attack against Ewell's judgment. As the case arose, and as the facts were, there can be no question that this was an unfortunate decision. Lee was aware of the advance of Slocum's corps to the support of the Federals, and knew that his own army was not yet concentrated, but that, in all probability, it would be concentrated more effectively than the Federals could be by the following morning. This was the evidence before him at the time, and the reasoning to be inferred from it, under all the circumstances of the case, leads one to think that he was justified in postponing the attack as he did. If Lee had then known what we now know, it may be assumed that he would have attacked; but had we been in his position then, it is tolerably certain that most generals would have done as he did. It is not by the knowledge we now have of all the circumstances that such a decision as that of Lee must be judged, but by the knowledge of the facts which he himself then possessed. That this knowledge was not more accurate was, no doubt, due to the previous absence of Stuart and his cavalry. It was the only campaign of the war in which Lee fought blindfold, and he bitterly paid the penalty for so fighting. It would be rather interesting to know whether disappointment at losing the precious opportunity did or did not, during the following days, somewhat affect the vigor of Ewell's coöperation. Something of the usual energy of the Confederates seems to have been missing on that side, and though it may be attributed chiefly to the delay and the uncertainty of the hour of Longstreet's attack, other causes probably contributed, and this disappointment on Ewell's part was most likely among them.

There seems to be this general peculiarity about these campaigns in the West—that they were fought very much to secure recruiting districts. Where the condition of feeling was such that it made all the difference whether the district was in the occupation of the Federal or the Confederate troops, and whether the

State authorities were in sympathy with Washington or Richmond, it is obvious that the conditions are very unlike those which usually obtain in European warfare. The only very analogous wars to which one can go back for similar conditions in this respect are those of Wallenstein and Gustavus Adolphus. Gustavus, when he died, left to his successor several armies, though he had entered Germany with but one. It made all the difference that he had been able to clear the Protestant districts of the Imperial troops, and to establish recruiting depots there. It is obvious that the wisdom of military movements, and the relative importance of certain campaigns, cannot, under these circumstances, be judged on precisely the same principles on which one would judge contests between the different nations in Europe.

If the statements as to the condition of popular sentiment in California and in the West during the earlier years of the war, which are furnished us in some of these papers, are to be relied upon, it is evident that the so-called New Mexican campaign was a much more important matter, small as were the forces engaged in it, than it has been supposed to be. As General Grant has said, the Confederacy, without large territories to extend into, was doomed, even if it succeeded in establishing its independence. It looks as if, but for the judicious arrangements made by the Federal commander, the Confederate forces, after their successes at San Augustine Springs and Valverde, might have formed an imposing army in New Mexico and Texas. Such an army, if properly supported from Richmond, might have enabled the various Confederate sympathizers to make head in California, and to secure the all-important Pacific Coast, with its important gold supply. It is scarcely possible to overrate the difference which that would have made in the conditions of the war. Probably the Confederacy, cut off as it was from all the outside world by the original mistakes of Mr. Davis's administration, could not have afforded to furnish supplies for this New Mexico campaign. But considering the initial success which attended it, and that it failed almost entirely from lack of material resources, one is led to think it would have been worth a more serious effort.

The junction of Van Dorn and Price with General Beauregard's forces, after the battle of Shiloh and the retreat from Corinth, seems to show clearly how easy would have been that junction in the mode suggested in my first article, prior to the

Pea Ridge campaign and the battle of Shiloh. Then it would, in all probability, have been decisive as far as the battle of Shiloh itself was concerned, and at least for the year it would have left the whole West in the hands of the Confederacy. Considering the state of feeling prevailing at that time, it is impossible to gauge what might not have been the effect in the creation of new Southern forces. The retreat from Corinth seems to have been an extremely skilfully-contrived movement on the part of General Beauregard. General Halleck appears to have done about as little as it was possible for a man to do with the imposing forces and the able soldiers, Grant, Sherman, and Sheridan, who were with him. The regathering of the Confederate forces at Tupelo, and the scattering of the great Union Army, are among the most curious incidents of the war. General Beauregard had done great things for the army under his command during the halt at Corinth and Tupelo. Under his fostering care it had vastly improved both in discipline and in military training. It was a Confederate misfortune when ill-health obliged him to leave and hand over command to General Bragg. The whole of Bragg's ill-advised invasion of Kentucky and the simultaneous movements which led to the battles of Iuka and Corinth, in September and October, 1862, can, it seems, be only justly judged by taking into account the question of the recruiting districts. Bragg's advance into Kentucky was a mere flash in the pan, not because of any strategical or tactical considerations, in the ordinary sense of the term, but because Kentucky did not rise in support of the Confederate cause. Whatever may have been the reason,—whether the actual amount of anti-Union feeling in the State had been exaggerated, or because, as Bragg thought, the blue-grass region was too rich to allow men readily to sacrifice their wealth and ease for any cause,—the fact remains that Bragg's invasion was undertaken to gain recruiting districts; that is, in other words, to afford the people of Kentucky the chance of rising in support of Southern independence. The attempt was a failure; the people did not enlist even in sufficient numbers to make up the waste which the campaign itself entailed. It is, therefore, difficult to see how any change in the handling of troops could have made much difference in the final result. "The people have too many fat cattle and are too well off to fight," was General Bragg's commentary upon the conduct of the Kentuckians.

Van Dorn's movement on Corinth to make a direct attack upon it, instead of manœuvring Rosecrans out of it, was a mistake that seems obvious on the face of the facts. When Bragg had been intrusted with the chief command in the district, it was an enormous blunder on the part of the Confederate Government to place Price's forces under the command of Van Dorn. This arrangement, made without notice, suddenly deprived Bragg of the support upon which he had counted ; that is clear enough. It distinctly violated the principle so well expressed afterwards by President Lincoln, that it is not wise " to swap horses whilst you are crossing a stream." As far as one can now judge of the relations of time and place, there was not time, it would seem, for Price to have moved with considerable effect upon Nashville, as Bragg had ordered him to do. At all events, his long circuitous movement to join Van Dorn was a waste of force, even apart from the disastrous termination of that movement in the battle of Corinth (October 4, 1862). Buell's army was exposed to very serious risk in the movement from Nashville upon Louisville, and that risk would have been greatly increased if Price had moved as rapidly as possible upon Nashville. General Bragg was a commander who seems to have been very uncertain in his action. At times he was both skilful in his arrangements and enterprising in his movements. Suddenly his skill deserted him at the most critical moments. During his bold but useless invasion of Kentucky, he was, no doubt, right in considering that everything depended on a proper coöperation between him and General Kirby Smith. No doubt the authorities at Richmond were largely to blame for not definitely appointing one man to command the joint expedition from the moment the invasion of Kentucky had been determined upon. Nevertheless, from the evidence before us, it seems clear that Bragg was supplied with sufficient information as to Buell's move to have enabled him to fall upon Buell's flank during his march from Nashville to Louisville.

The decisive effect of such a move was so obvious that Bragg would clearly have been able to call upon General Smith to support him, and the junction of the two forces ought to have been made by Smith's junction with Bragg rather than by Bragg joining Smith. It is difficult to see how, if Bragg, supported as rapidly as possible by Smith, had fallen upon Buell during the march,—still more, if simultaneously, as Bragg wished, Price had moved upon Nashville, instead of moving round to join Van Dorn at Corinth,—Nashville or Louisville could have escaped falling into the hands of the Confederate generals. Probably in that case they would have been able to strike back in time to intercept the retreat of the Union force from Cumberland Gap. If, as the Confederate writers seem to believe, the effect of so great a success would have been to induce Kentucky to throw itself heartily into the cause of the South, the result would have been most important. Without that, it is obvious that just as Lee's invasion of Pennsylvania caused numbers of the local militia to come to the aid of the Union forces, so the approach of Bragg's army to the borders of Ohio and Indiana tended to raise fresh armies against him. No doubt much of the relative ill-success, in proportion to numbers, which subsequently attended Buell's movement may be attributed to the rawness of that general's troops, who were little better than mere recruits, whilst Bragg's men had been trained to war in several campaigns. In the action of Perryville (October 8, 1862), which followed upon Buell's gradual concentration of force at Louisville, and the consequent retreat of Bragg, Buell evidently succeeded in imposing upon Bragg as to the direction in which he intended to move. Bragg's success in the fight and his successful retreat afterwards appear to have been very much the result of his possessing an army much better in hand and more experienced in fighting than it was possible for Buell to have collected under the circumstances at the time.

Though not prepared to modify the opinion expressed elsewhere, that General Lee was the most remarkable man the Civil War produced, and though I cannot admit that General Grant possessed at all the same genius for command, yet it must be at once confessed that it is an immense relief to turn from the mirage of these indecisive battles and movements in the West to the story of the Vicksburg campaign. It is very natural that General Sherman should rate very highly the military genius of General Grant, for the great services which, in the summer of 1863, Grant rendered to the Union made him tower head and shoulders over all others who could possibly be placed in supreme command of the Federal armies. McClellan had become by this time a political character, and as long as Mr. Lincoln remained President it was impossible that he should be again appointed Commander-in-Chief. The elections had already begun to show the effect which the depression caused by Fredericksburg and Chancellorsville was producing throughout the North. Halleck, applying to a campaign which he could not stop till its success was assured the mischievous interference which had been in the East so fruitful in disaster, at last palpably stultified himself, even in the eyes of the President and the Cabinet. The scheme of the Vicksburg campaign was both original and brilliant in conception, and vigorous and fortunate in execution. Sherman, loyally anxious to acknowledge his own opposition to it, contributed, no doubt, largely to cause the military skill which Grant had shown to be appreciated throughout the country.

In its general character of sudden movement, by which he enlisted on the side of his army the advantages of surprise by a concentrated force, unentangled by any line of supplies, the Vicksburg campaign closely resembles many of Jackson's operations. It had something of the character of his campaign in the Shenandoah Valley, and something that recalled his movements which preceded the second Bull Run. The news of such strokes as Grant delivered in rapid succession at Port Gibson, South Fork, Fourteen-Mile Creek, Raymond, Jackson, Champion's Hill, and Big Black River, coming at a moment when gold had gone up to a figure hitherto unknown, and in the very weeks which immediately succeeded Chancellorsville and preceded Lee's invasion of Pennsylvania, must, indeed, have seemed like a sudden break of light through the darkest of clouds. No wonder, therefore, that public attention became concentrated on the siege of Vicksburg. The very fact that six weeks elapsed before the surrender was probably in favor of Grant's reputation. It gave time for representative people from the North to gather in the besieger's lines, and hear from the victorious army all the particulars about the successful campaign, and to learn how entirely it depended for its conception and execution upon the skill of one man, and upon the confidence which he had inspired in his subordinates.

When, almost at the same moment, the fall of Vicksburg and the battle of Gettysburg made the 4th of July, 1863, almost a new birthday for the Union, the general self-congratulation of th ! North made all hearts crave for a hero—for some one in whom o feel confidence. All this tended greatly, and very naturally, to increase the importance of Grant's position. In the West, che work accomplished and the victories achieved were pal ibly

Grant's own, but from the first the general public, at least, seem to have refused to Meade the honors of the battle which had been won under his orders. When, in consequence of the defeat at Chickamauga, the virtual investment of Rosecrans's army in Chattanooga, and the unhappy condition of Burnside's army at Knoxville, the aspect of affairs in the West again became gloomy and threatening, it followed as a matter of course that General Grant should be intrusted with the task of restoring the Union affairs in the West.

General Bragg seems to have shown, in the campaigns which had intervened since his retreat from Kentucky, a strange mixture of qualities. At the battle of Stone's River he successfully planned and carried out an attack upon the right flank of Rosecrans's army. But when everything was going in his favor, he abandoned his advantage, and, instead of crushing in the defeated wing upon the other wing, made a gratuitous attack upon the strongest intact position left to the enemy, and at a point where his previous success gave him no advantage. Rosecrans skilfully manœuvred Bragg out of his defensive positions, and forced him back beyond Chattanooga in June and July, 1863. The art of finding out the position, movements, and intentions of the enemy is the A B C of generalship. Of this art General Bragg was not only ignorant, but he lacked even the power to put together into one intelligible whole the information daily supplied by his outposts and obtained from other sources. At Chickamauga the victory was clearly in no way due to Bragg, and his incapacity to realize the nature of the situation presented to him was very much alike at the two battles of Stone's River and Chickamauga. He seems in the first instance to have contrived with considerable skill the virtual investment of Rosecrans in Chattanooga, but it is difficult to understand why, if his force was sufficient to allow him to detach Longstreet at all, he should not have attacked Bridgeport before the arrival of Hooker's troops. To have done so would have deprived the Union troops of their only means of constructing boats within reach of the beleaguered army. Bragg seems to have relapsed into a condition of careless confidence after the important positions round Chattanooga had been, in the first instance, secured. So much so that things were left in a condition which only required that a vigorous leader should restore confidence to the army of the Union to make it certain that the besiegers would lose all the results of their previous successes. So far as one may judge from the papers contributed to this series, those who fought under Grant at Chattanooga are by no means disposed to credit him with any great share in the work of opening the "cracker line," or even in planning the battle itself. I am disposed to think that they hardly do General Grant justice. It may be very true that the apparently splendid effect which, as the broad results only were heard of at a distance, appeared to attend the placing of Grant in command of the army and the dismissal of Rosecrans, was something of a *coup de théâtre*. It may be very true that the arrangements for opening communications had been at least partly planned under Rosecrans before Grant's arrival at Chattanooga, on the 23d October, 1863, and that they were mainly the work of subordinates. It may be true that, in the actual moment of victory at that place, the successful charge of Thomas was due to the spontaneous enthusiasm of the men, and that it was actually carried out in excess of Grant's intention or order. If it be assumed that Grant trusted entirely for his success to Sherman's attack upon the Confederate right, or trusted for success even to the combined effect of Sherman's and of Hooker's movement, it is no doubt true that Grant's original plan was not carried out. Grant certainly made many changes in his plans of attack, but surely this sort of criticism is not by any means fair to a general commanding an army in battle! The changes of plans seem to have been only such as the changing circumstances rendered necessary. General Grant acknowledges that Rosecrans offered him many most valuable suggestions, and rather pithily says : "My only surprise was that he had not carried them out." This may or may not be quite fair to Rosecrans, and it may be the case that the arrangements were being worked out as rapidly as circumstances admitted before Grant's arrival. But, taking the whole of the facts as they stand, it seems clear that while Grant, as any sensible man in his case would have done, took advantage of whatever had been effected before his arrival that promised to be useful, and listened to all suggestions that were likely to assist in the solution of a very difficult problem, nevertheless it was his energy and skill which carried the whole of the scheme through the great victory of Chattanooga. No doubt, as continually occurs in war, things did not happen exactly in the way he had designed they should happen, but he was ready to do the best thing that was to be done under all the fresh circumstances as they arose. The actual working-out, the general superintendence of the whole scheme, were his and his alone.

The panic which appears at the last in that battle to have seized upon a portion of the Confederate Army was not, I think, the improbable event General Bragg seems to have considered it. Nothing tells so much on the confidence and courage of an army as the conviction that their general has been outmanœuvred by the enemy. Now, his army, it seems, never had any very special confidence in Bragg, and every misfortune is possible to the army that has no confidence in its leader. The battle of Chickamauga, and the knowledge that he had actually absented himself from the field under the belief that the battle was lost, must have greatly diminished their faith in him, even in the moment of victory. Then, after their successful investment of the Union army in Chattanooga, with everything to raise their spirits and depress those of their opponents, there came upon them one blow after another; first, the opening of the "cracker line," which meant, as they well knew, that there was no longer any hope of seeing the Federal Army surrender from want of food and ammunition; then the successive reënforcements of the Federals, the arrival of Hooker and of Sherman, the most unwise withdrawal of Longstreet's force, and of the detachments sent afterwards to reënforce him, just before Grant was ready to attack. Then came the successful ruse and surprise by which Thomas carried the outposts and picket-lines of the besiegers, and took up a threatening position all along the front of their works; then General Hooker, by the successful employment of superior forces against a weak part of the Confederate line, necessitated the withdrawal of their troops from Lookout Mountain; and then came Sherman's successful surprise of their pickets on the right, by means of which he contrived to get his troops across the river without loss, and to establish them, unknown to his enemy, on their right flank.

I think one may well guess what must have been the effect of all these Federal operations upon the minds of the Confederate soldiers. It is quite true that little material advantage was actually gained by Grant by his attack on the Chattanooga position. But each succeeding event tended to depress the spirits of the

Confederate Army, to shake their confidence in their leaders, whilst, on the other hand, every fresh move of Grant's tended to restore confidence to the Federal troops, and to make them believe they were being skilfully led. There is a sense in which, with armies as with individuals, deep depression, when once relieved, tends to pass rapidly into a condition of high exaltation, all the more effective because of the reaction from the previous opposite feeling. The army under the command of General Thomas, after all the misery and starvation they had courageously endured, seem to have passed through these phases. Nothing could have been better calculated to excite in them an extreme and passionate desire to go through any sacrifice for victory than that they should be kept for some time idly waiting in front of the enemy, whose forward position they had already seized, and compelled to witness the fighting being done for them by the armies that had come to relieve them—by Sherman on their left, and by Hooker on their right.

Those are circumstances under which you may securely trust Anglo-Saxon troops, at least when once released from the leash, to go forward, as those of General Thomas did, with a bound that carries everything before it, and that probably exceeds both your wishes and your orders. The apparently-sudden change in temperament of their opponents seems to have been all that was needed to convert the discouragement of the Southerners into actual flight. Grant certainly deserves all possible credit for having, within the time between his arrival and the battle of Chattanooga, done so much thus to change the condition of the *morale* of his own army, and of that which was opposed to it. He further deserves the credit of having realized how important that change was to him, and how advantage could best be taken of it. The story told in these papers is a fitting introduction to the time when Grant was to be transferred to a yet higher command, and to be pitted against very different opponents from Generals Bragg and Pemberton.

It is rather curious that this third volume on the Civil War should close with an account of Longstreet's first independent command, in which, far from remaining perpetually on the defensive, he committed himself to the particularly bloody attack upon Knoxville, which, ill-prepared and ill-advised, ended in failure. WOLSELEY.

[TO BE CONTINUED.]

ERICSSON AND HIS "MONITOR."

BY CHARLES W. MACCORD, SC.D., PROFESSOR OF MECHANICAL DRAWING, STEVENS INSTITUTE OF TECHNOLOGY. (FORMERLY CHIEF DRAUGHTSMAN FOR CAPTAIN JOHN ERICSSON.)

THE 8th of March twenty-seven years ago has become historic as a day of defeat and gloomy portent, when the sinking of the "Cumberland" and the burning of the "Congress" destroyed at a blow all confidence in the strength of our navy, and spread dismay at the defenceless condition of our seacoast towns.

And by the association of ideas the 8th of March is still more strongly emphasized; it is the black-letter day on the calendar of the present year, for then the busy brain of the world's most illustrious engineer ceased forever from its labors. The events of the earlier time are vividly recalled by the death of Ericsson, whose name will always have something of magic in it; for it was he who enabled us to retrieve that reverse, who lifted the pall of despondency which overshadowed the land, and did more than any other single man to preserve the integrity of the Union. The speediness of the revenge, too, fitly harmonized with his energetic nature; on the very next day, in the very same place, while seeking new victories, the conqueror met defeat; not in a dream, and scarcely by a miracle, could the dramatic effect have been enhanced.

Nor is there upon record a coincidence more striking or more suggestive: in the darkness of the early morning, the great designer set sail upon the unknown sea, on the anniversary of the very day when his little ship had come to anchor in the roadstead, in the darkness of the evening,—a darkness soon to be dispelled by the splendors of a triumph, which for all coming time has fixed his name and hers in golden letters upon the tablets of our history.

The story of the "Monitor's" building has been often told: the fertility of invention, facility in designing, speed and accuracy in drawing, promptness in execution, and unwearied industry which made the construction possible in so short a time— all these are familiar. But the minor mishaps, the special incidents which, apparently adverse, yet proved providential as contributing to that exact coincidence of time, place, and circumstance upon which so much depended—these have as yet been omitted in the telling, and without them the story is incomplete.

While the vessel was on the stocks, Captain Ericsson made frequent and for a part of the time daily visits to the yard of the Continental Works, watching operations with a keen and critical eye; but after the launch he considered this no longer necessary, and visited her but seldom. In this way it came about that, although the motive engines were put in before launching, he did not see them under steam, but contented himself with the reports of their action made by the government engineers. These engines were of what has ever since been called the "Monitor type," and many have supposed that they were, like the vessel itself, of wholly novel and untried design. This, however, was not the case. In the "Judith" and the "Daylight," and elsewhere, this form of engine had already demonstated its practical working qualities: otherwise the captain would probably have given the first trials at the dock his personal supervision.

For obvious reasons, as little publicity as possible had been given to the work during its progress, but perfect secrecy was, of course, out of the question. The turret of a monitor can not be hidden under a bushel, nor could the launching of an iron-clad vessel be concealed from the public eye; and, indeed, it had been watched by some in expectation that this strange craft, built in defiance of everything considered ship-shape, apparently overweighted with iron, and with no free-board worth mentioning, would slide off the ways straight to the bottom of the East River and never come up again. Disappointed of this sensation, the public had manifested no little curiosity to see how the "Ericsson Battery" would behave when she left the dock. This curiosity was soon gratified; the final preparations were pushed with unabated vigor, and, the engines having been reported in satisfactory working order, upon one gloomy winter's day a formal trial trip was made.

The result of this trial was anything but encouraging, as reported in the daily papers, one of which made it the text of a "crushing" article, wherein, under the heading of "ERICSSON'S FOLLY," the battery was pronounced an ignominious failure, which could neither be propelled nor steered; the captain was called an incapable schemer, and a stern reproof was given for the sin of thus wasting the country's resources;—no words too harsh, no denunciations too severe, for the zeal of this fiery crusader. The versatility of the modern journalist stood him in good stead on the 10th of March, when the novel fighting machine had proved invulnerable to heavier blows than his pen could deal; but in the meantime it must be admitted that the battery had not behaved as well as she might. The motive engines were not in proper adjustment, the steering-gear required excessive power, and between the two the vessel proved unmanageable; the trial was given up, and she had to be towed back—a rude disappointment indeed to expectations which no one conversant with all the facts can regard as unreasonable.

It is well known that John Ericsson was by nature sanguine and enthusiastic; impetuous, excitable, and impatient of contradiction, with him it was "*Sic volo, sic jubeo, stet pro ratione voluntas*"; nor did he always in the heat of the moment consider whether his wishes could be executed by those not endowed with his own tireless energy. The events of that dismal day must have vexed his very soul, but the manner in which he bore them was strikingly characteristic. Had they been trifling things, he would have been exasperated, as his custom was, and exasperating, too, when small affairs went wrong; but under heavy burdens his broad shoulders never bent, and he looked always squarely in the face of grave misfortunes with calm and resolute eyes. It is true that on his return to Franklin Street, where he then resided, there was a somewhat portentous cloud upon his face, and no wonder; but it was not the forerunner of a storm.

At his request I brought the drawings of the valve gear, not without misgivings, for he had never examined them with a view to verification, and I alone was responsible for their accuracy. He wanted the plan showing the relative positions of the eccentrics and the main crank; and I was obliged to explain that I had no original, having made the working tracing, in order to save time, from detached drawings and a pencil diagram. He listened with patience and appeared satisfied with my detailed explanation, and then requested me to make a new drawing of the complete arrangement, trace it, and as soon as possible to call in the old plan, give out the new one, and give orders to have the eccentrics at once set according to it. I was then informed that during all the trials at the dock the engines had been running *backward*, of which Chief-Engineer Stimers, who, it seems, had never inquired whether the propeller were right-handed or left-handed, was not aware. Simple reversal would not, at best, have fully met the difficulty; for each slide valve was driven by a loose eccentric, which was shifted part way round in order to reverse—an arrangement which, if adjusted to give the best results in one direction, will not in that type of engine do equally well in the other. Still this could not have been the whole secret, though it was never discovered just what was; for the subsequent difference between the forward and backward running was never great enough to have caused so much trouble; and, again, the same device was used in many engines of the same form afterward, about which no complaint was made.

Be that as it may, I did not feel like taking the responsibility of giving out the new plan without his scrutiny; but he would not look at it, only saying: "You are sure it is right now? Very well; then go ahead." I did so, and, having captured the first tracing, lost no time in comparing it with the new drawing; to my great relief, they tallied exactly, so that both tracings might have been made from the same original plan.

Some time after, meeting the superintendent of the Delamater Works, I tried to ascertain the real cause of the difficulty, but without success. He asserted that the first drawings of the valve gear were all wrong, admitted that the new ones were all right, and averred that the plans had been carefully followed in both cases. After a brief explanation, I invited him to accompany me to No. 95 Franklin Street and compare the old with the new; but he found that he had not time. Captain Ericsson had once described this superintendent as "too stupid to make a blunder," which only proves that his own judgment was not infallible; but whatever the precise nature or cause of this annoying maladjustment, it is absolutely certain that it was due to no error or oversight at headquarters. And it was so quickly rectified that the trifling delay arising from this cause alone would not have prevented the "Monitor" from meeting her adversary before the eventful 9th of March.

She had become unmanageable, not only from the temporary failure of her engines, but from want of control over her steering-gear. The cause of this was that her rudder was somewhat overbalanced; the area forward of the rudder-post being too great in proportion to that aft of it. In these circumstances, the rudder, once thrown over to either side, does not readily return, but opposes considerable resistance to any effort to bring it back to its central position. Those who choose may attribute this to miscalculation; but it is for them to prove that under all the conditions, known and unknown, the exact proportion which shall require the least power can be determined by any known means. At any rate, there was the hard, uncomfortable fact; it was not the hour, nor was Ericsson the man, to indulge in idle speculations as to how or why it came there; but had he adopted the remedy suggested to him, it is morally certain that the battle between the giant and the pygmy would not have occurred when and where it did.

This remedy was neither more nor less than the replacing of the balanced rudder by one of different form. I do not know where the idea originated, nor do I say that any formal proposal was made, but in some way the captain became aware of an intention of the naval authorities to have the vessel put in the dry-dock and fitted with a new rudder. The hot Scandinavian blood flushed his cheek, his eyes gleamed, his brow darkened ; and this time the storm broke in all its fury. With the full volume of his tremendous voice, and with a mighty oath, he thundered: "The 'Monitor' is MINE, and I say it shall not be done." Presently he added, in a tone of supreme contempt: "Put in a new rudder! They would waste a month in doing that; I will make her steer just as easily in three days."

My recollection is that it was done in less time. No change in the rudder was even thought of, and the change in the steering-gear was the simplest possible. Her tiller consisted of an arc of iron, with two angle-irons on the outer side ; round each of these was wound a chain, which, running around a pulley below the deck, was attached to a wire tiller-rope leading forward to the pilot-house, and coiled in the usual manner round the drum of the steering-wheel. By Captain Ericsson's direction, the wire ropes were now detached from the chains, to each of which a snatch-block was made fast; a short chain was connected at one end to each tiller-rope, run through one of these blocks, brought back parallel to itself, and secured at the other end to a deck-beam. The purchase being thus doubled, the trouble was over and the vessel steered with ease.

Considering how precious were the moments then, the suggestion of a new rudder might well excite his indignation and disgust. But the captain's wrath was chiefly roused by the idea of any official interference with the vessel as yet unpaid for and wholly in his own hands; which was perfectly natural in view of his treatment by the government in this and other matters. It will be always recorded in the history of this country that the building of the "Monitor" was sanctioned by the authorities at Washington only upon conditions the most arbitrary and, in the circumstances, the most contemptible, ever imposed by a great government upon a great designer. At a price barely sufficient to cover the cost of materials and labor, they would accept his battery, but not until it had proved impregnable under the guns of the enemy at the shortest range; in a most critical emergency, they would take all the profit if he would take all the risk. Twenty years before, these United States had reaped the fruit of his genius and his labor, when the building of the "Princeton" had also marked a new era in naval construction. During all those years they had refused, as they have refused during all the longer years since, to pay him for his services, although in the meantime there had been days when the paltry sum would have been most acceptable; they are willing, it seems, that the memory of their meanness shall be everlasting, since they have allowed him to carry it with him to his eternal rest.

Nevertheless, as then in time of peace he had prepared them for war, so now in time of war he was ready to prepare them for peace, and that upon their own one-sided, almost humiliating, terms. To accept those terms was an act of magnanimity, and a proof, were any needed, that what he soon after said to me was true,—"I love this country. I love its people and its laws; and I would give my life for it just as soon as not." Patriotic he was, but also he was proud; the sting of the earlier injustice still rankled, and it was only at the earnest solicitation of a friend that he consented to appear in Washington to demonstrate that he was conferring a boon, not soliciting a favor. But for which it might not have happened that in this country and for this country were built the two most conspicuous of the many monuments of his genius that mark his path all the way from the cottage in Vermland to the halls of Valhalla.

The trial of the armament also contributed its quota to the general result, in a manner which proved to be amusing, though the consequences narrowly escaped being disastrous. It must first be explained that the friction for taking up the recoil was produced by means of two levers, actuated by a screw, with a hand-wheel at the side of the gun-carriage. Since there were two guns, pointing in the same direction, with very little space between them, the hand-wheels were, of course, placed on the outer sides of the carriages; naturally suggesting the idea that the whole mechanism was right-handed for one and left-handed for the other. But this was not so; in order to save time it was made the same for each, and in serving either gun the compression was effected by turning the top of the wheel to the left. Now, screws are ordinarily turned the other way in order to produce pressure; and Chief-Engineer Stimers, by whom the trial was conducted, would seem not to have made himself acquainted with the construction here adopted. Grasping the hand-wheel of gun No. 1, he turned it *to the right* until the resistance in his judgment indicated a proper degree of compression, and gave the order to fire. It must next be stated that the first effect of his action was to relieve any pressure that might have existed; the second effect was that the levers, whose movement was quite limited, became jammed in the supporting brackets, thus causing the resistance which had completely deceived the chief engineer. The great weapon gave a sullen roar, and, being entirely free, flew back until it was stopped by the cascabel striking against the interior of the turret.

One would imagine this experience sufficient to inspire caution; but, curiously enough, Engineer Stimers seems to have assumed that the carriages must be rights and lefts, and to have concluded that what was thus proved wrong for one was exactly the correct thing for the other. And so, without looking under the gun to see what was there and make sure of what he was really doing, he at once proceeded to experiment with gun No. 2 in the same manner, and with precisely similar results. Thus both guns were temporarily disabled, though, strange to say, neither was dismounted, nor were the carriages broken. The actual damage was surprisingly small, consisting chiefly in the shearing off of some bolts which secured the bearings of the guide rollers to the carriages; these, however, were not easily accessible, and the repairs necessarily consumed some little time.

Now, it may be safely said that without the occurrence of these things, or of any one of them, the course of affairs at that critical period would have been materially changed. The minor as well as the major planets must be consulted in casting the horoscope, and trivial as such incidents might seem in ordinary times, each had its share in fixing the day and the hour of a mighty contest, and the fortunes of a nation depended on the twist of a screw-thread. By far the most important one, as measured by its possible consequences, was the trouble with the steering-gear, though from the simplicity of the remedy it might appear the most insignificant; and it was this that brought into the boldest relief the prominent traits of the captain's character His keen mechanical instinct, quick decision, firmness of resolve, his fiery spirit, his energy in action, were all conspicuous; but all these were dominated by self-reliance and his pride in originality.

He loved to do his own work in his own way, and his fertility of expedient was something marvellous; to quote his own words on another occasion, "If I ever do get into a scrape, I know exactly how to get out of it"; and men unlike him, as most men are, were more likely than he to follow the lines laid down by others. He had said, "The 'Monitor' is mine," and his she was, in another and to him a far dearer sense; from turret to keel-plate, from rudder-shoe to anchor-well, every distinctive feature was the creation of his brain; every detail was stamped with the evidence of his handiwork. It was he who had planned the mechanism which had sulkily refused to obey his will, and he, or no man, should dictate the change which would reduce it to subjection. How much we owe to this one instance of determined resolution it is not easy to say. It prevented a fatal delay at a momentous crisis, and was thus the cause of that unparalleled change in national feeling which followed, when in every hamlet it was told, "The Ericsson Battery has saved the Union." It seized the golden moment of opportunity; it changed defeat into victory—victory which revolutionized naval warfare, wrung from England the reluctant admission, "Yesterday we had a great navy; to-day we have but two war-ships worthy of the name," and compelled our own government to exhibit a tardy confidence in the genius of the man whom it has persistently wronged. A grim testimonial of the fact that this confidence was not misplaced lies in the Royal Museum at Stockholm—a fifteen-inch shell with this significant inscription:

GUSTAVUS VASA FOX
Fann denna kula bland Sumters ruiner. *

And it would have been well had either of two other things been done as he wished. He had hoped for fifteen-inch guns; but they could not be procured in time. The largest available were eleven-inch, from which were fired only shells, with a service charge of fifteen pounds; against which the armor of the "Merrimac" was just strong enough to be proof. Foreseeing this, he had provided wrought-iron solid shot, to be used with a greater charge: not one was fired. The occasion would have warranted some little advance on previous practice, even if not advised by so thorough an expert as Captain Ericsson unquestionably was; that it was not made was no fault of either officers or crew, than whom no braver men ever trod a deck or served a gun; and the soundness of his judgment was proved by the subsequent use of double the quantity of powder. Had the government been able to furnish the heavier guns, or its officials been willing to sanction the heavier charges, there is little doubt that the "Merrimac" would have been quickly sent to keep company with her victims.

This had seemed to the captain so surely attainable with the means at hand that he could not regard the actual result with pleasure wholly unalloyed. Still it brought him a triumphant vindication of his bold defiance of precedent, the proud consciousness of a great service rendered to the country of his choice, the applause of a startled world, the enthusiastic gratitude of half a continent. Well might a feeling of elation take

* Gustavus Vasa Fox found this shot in the ruins of Sumter.

full possession of mind and soul, and overcome for the time not only the will, but the power, to pursue ordinary vocations. But no ordinary man was here: exultant, proud, and happy he was—no one who saw him could doubt that; but his steadfast mind did not swerve from the even tenor of its path, nor were his usual occupations interrupted for a single day. The fighting ability of the turret ship was established beyond a question, but her sea-going qualities were still held in doubt; and hardly had the echoes died away in Hampton Roads before he sat down quietly to plan a fleet of still greater pugnacious power; one of which, besides, was yet to round Cape Horn and enter the Golden Gate, another to visit his native Sweden and anchor under the guns of Cronstadt, while a third, sent to sea like a child in leading-strings, under the care of an escort, repaid the motherly attention by towing her disabled convoy safely into port;—and thus it was proved that the monitors were fully competent to take care of themselves, of their enemies, and of their friends.

The captain was disappointed that the "Monitor" had not done her utmost during the engagement; by her subsequent inactivity he was simply enraged. He was, himself, the active voice incarnate, and the passive voice was to him absolutely incomprehensible; like the hot and angry bee, who never rests, and wonders how others can, he saw in the end of one task only the beginning of another. He had built his ship to *fight;* and I never heard him allude to the "excessive caution" which kept her idle after her one battle, without scathing denunciations couched in language as fluent as it was vigorous, and more uncomplimentary than either. Both things appear the more to be regretted in the light of subsequent events, since they afforded a pretext for the shameless tirade of Winter Davis, who said: "The 'Monitor' and the 'Merrimac' met by accident in Hampton Roads; neither whipped, and the world went wild over two guns in a cheese-box." To be sure, the point is taken out of this sting when the armaments are compared; ten guns against two is heavy odds, and there would have been enough to admire had the smaller vessel but held her own. And though our own excited people might easily make an exaggerated estimate of the result, the spectators often judge the game better that the interested players, and the world at large does not go wild over a drawn battle. Still the shallow orator spoke more truly than he knew or meant when he said they met by chance, for though the "Monitor" was designed expressly to fight the "Merrimac," their meeting then and there hinged upon circumstances which were, humanly speaking, accidental, if anything ever was.

It is not suprising that the fervor of an enthusiasm caused by such sudden and unexpected deliverance from impending disaster should, in a manner, overdo itself, and give rise to expectations altogether too extravagant to be realized, nor yet that this should be followed by a reaction; a populace, with proverbial fickleness, unduly depreciating what had before been, perhaps, too highly extolled. But whatever may be said in extenuation of utterances made while feelings and opinions were thus fluctuating, nothing can be urged upon such grounds after the normal level has been resumed. Still it is sometimes said now, as it was often said then, in a derogatory sense, that Captain Ericsson made many mistakes, and that he persistently refused to accept the suggestions of others. It cannot be denied that both these things are true, but the recoil of this weapon is its only dangerous feature; for due account must be taken of the new and original work which he accomplished, thereby making himself a tremendous factor in the material progress of the world during the present century. He was versatile and prolific in ideas to an extent seldom approached, his work being no less remarkable for its variety than for its intrinsic importance, while its amount was simply astounding; so that its execution, even with his unrivalled celerity, would have been impossible without uninterrupted application. Plenty there were who were willing, many much more than they were able, to give advice. Had he taken time to listen to it all, the record of what he has done would have been much shorter than it is.

Mistakes he made, and he knew it; his projects were not always successful. In exploring new fields, errors are often found assuming the garb of truth so effectually that the imposition is not at once detected; in the development of new ideas perfection is seldom reached without repeated trials; and to say that the captain made mistakes is simply to affirm that he was human; but when they are compared with the total results of his labors, the ratio is so small that no one has yet laid stress upon them who would not, in the caustic words of John Bourne, "have been a much more distinguished engineer than he is if he had never done anything in his life except to contrive the mistakes of Ericsson."

I have already alluded to a protest made against "the wasting of the people's money" before the first of the monitors was completed. It is singular enough that, when the last of them had been for years out of commission, the same stupid cry of indignation was repeated in reference to the highly-finished machinery of the largest of the turret ships. The absurdity of the first complaint was very soon made evident; and the second was equally without foundation, for the money thus expended was not the people's money. But what if it had been? Who, I ask, in the name of all that is just, of all that is generous, of all that is patriotic, had a better right to waste a little of it, if waste it can be called, than the man who, at the risk of his own thousands, had saved the people from the loss of unknown millions?

Such utterances serve only to show the depths to which it is possible for little minds to descend. For the very lowest standard by which such works as his can be gauged is that of money value; and leaving out of the account the advances which he had already made in naval warfare, and considering only the effects of his previous career upon the peaceful arts, upon commercial enterprise, and general material prosperity, it is easy to show that the gain directly traceable to his single-handed exertions is great almost beyond computation. The people were very largely indebted to him for the magnitude of the interests at stake;—in a word, he had done more to develop this country than he did even to defend it. Either was a more than sufficient foundation for enduring fame, but with the latter his name will be always more closely associated by every true American; and simply as the builder of the "Monitor," it is safe to say that the memory of John Ericsson will be green in the minds of men long after not only carping criticisms, but the critics themselves, with their records, their achievements and all, shall have been sunk fathoms deep in the everlasting limbo of forgotten things.

CHARLES W. MACCORD.

LORD WOLSELEY'S MISTAKES.*

BY JEFFERSON DAVIS.

Lord Wolseley has twice conspicuously assumed the part of a self-appointed judge of certain military problems presented by the war between the States, and has presumed to pronounce his decisions in a tone of authority that, viewing his capacity, amuses, and, viewing his record, amazes, the reader competent to judge between the critic and the movements and men he has undertaken to criticise. In THE NORTH AMERICAN REVIEW for May he returns with increased venom to his attack on the Confederate Executive. As his reference to me is so manifestly dragged into his article, and so transparently an ebullition of temper, I had not intended to notice it. But I have been so earnestly urged by personal friends in both sections, in the interest of historical truth, to refute Lord Wolseley's slanderous perversions of Confederate history that I reluctantly yield my personal inclination to reply to him in the pages of THE REVIEW.

My reluctance to engage in the controversy relating to the war between the States is not personal only, but rests on considerations of public interest; for such controversies give occasion to demagogues for reviving old animosities that are injurious to the general welfare—animosities which, unless stimulated, will surely and speedily disappear. But, on the other hand, in order that crimination and recrimination between the States may forever cease, it is needful that the truth, and the whole truth, should be known, and not perverted in the interest of faction. An *entente cordiale* cannot rest on a partisan pedestal.

* * General Wolseley having criticised the Hon. Jefferson Davis in one of his articles, it seems but fair that the ex-President of the Confederacy should have an opportunity to reply. At the same time, it should be remembered, in justice to General Wolseley, that that distinguished soldier expressly states that his articles deal only with the information supplied by *The Century's* history of the Civil War; and he cannot be held responsible for deficiencies in that source of information.- EDITOR NORTH AMERICAN REVIEW.

For my own part in the contest between the sections I have no excuses to make and no apology to offer. I did my duty to the best of my ability, according to the faith in which I was reared and to which I adhere. What is true in my own case is equally true of my associates. Instead of being "traitors," we were loyal to our States; instead of being rebels against the Union, we were defenders of the Constitution as framed by its founders and as expounded by them. Taught by them to regard the State as sovereign and the Federal Government as the agent, not the ruler, of the State, we loyally followed the lead of the sovereign and resisted the usurpations of the agent. We do not fear the verdict of posterity on the purity of our motives or the sincerity of our belief, which our sacrifices and career sufficiently attested.

But while we of the South have no desire to keep alive the controversies of the war, it is equally due to our own self-respect and a duty to our dead associates to repel the unjust aspersions that it has been sought to fasten on the motives and conduct of the leaders of the Confederacy.

In previous attacks Lord Wolseley contented himself, as he does in the first few pages of his first NORTH AMERICAN REVIEW article, with speaking of me in a tone of lofty disparagement, without condescending to give specific reasons for his unfavorable opinion. But now, after a somewhat Olympian sentence of condemnation, the Adjutant-General incautiously gives a condensed bill of particulars, as if to justify his unfavorable opinion. He writes:

"It may be said that it was impossible for any one to foresee the dimensions to which the struggle would grow. But surely it is a statesman's business at least partially to gauge the strength of the forces with which he has to deal. The *soi-disant* statesman who began his high duties with the avowed expectation that 10,000 Enfield rifles would be sufficient to overawe the United States; who then refused the services of 366,000 men, the flower of the South, and accepted only a fraction of them, because he had not arms for more; the man who neglected to buy the East Indian fleet, which happy chance and the zeal of subordinates threw in his way; the ruler who could not see that the one vital necessity for the South was, at all sacrifice and at all hazard, to keep the ports open; who rejected all means proposed by others for placing the finances of the Confederacy on a sound basis,—that man, as I think, did more than any other individual on either side to save the Union. I have not attempted to make the charge against him as complete and crushing as it could easily be made by those who trusted him with almost unlimited powers in their behalf."

Specifications are always needed to give credence, if not currency, to false accusations against men in representative official positions; but as the acts of such men are necessarily of public record, they enjoy a facility of refutation rarely accorded to men in more private stations.

I might well be ashamed of my public career if I could feel that the opinion of any European stripling without an earned record of ability either in civil or military life could affect my reputation in America, and therefore I pass unnoticed his personal depreciation; but I should have graver cause to be ashamed of my administration of the Confederate Government if the allegations he makes, without proof or reference, were founded in fact.

Each and every allegation in Lord Wolseley's indictment, above quoted, is either false in direct statement or false by inference.

It is impossible, in the limited space you assign me, fully to refute all of Lord Wolseley's false statements by all the abundant proofs in contemporary records and books that I might easily submit; but in the restricted space placed at my disposal I shall notice each of his allegations as briefly as possible.

I.—*"The soi-disant statesman who began his high duties with the avowed expectation that 10,000 Enfield rifles would be sufficient to overawe the United States; who then refused the services of 366,000 men, the flower of the South, and accepted only a fraction of them, because he had not arms for more."*

This assertion that 366,000 men, "the flower of the South," were offered to me and refused is so devoid of truth or probability that only the most reckless indifference to both could have uttered it. That in the then condition of the Confederate States there should have been such a numerous organization to offer itself is as incredible as that the President, who notoriously differed with most of his countrymen in apprehending a long and bloody war, should have declined the services of such a force. It is untrue as a whole and in every part. A writer of history may be expected to consult contemporaneous records rather than to accept the rumors of manifestly unfriendly writers. In this case, for example, reference might have been made to the Confederate law of that period.

In the act of March 6, 1861, "to provide for the public defence," the first section authorized the President of the Confederate States of America to ask for and accept the services of any number of volunteers, not exceeding 100,000, "to serve for twelve months, unless sooner discharged." By the second section it is enacted that the volunteers, when mustered into service, should be armed by the States from which they came or by the Confederate States. By the fifth section the President was authorized to accept the volunteers in companies, squadrons, battalions, and regiments. From this it will be seen that the largest organization contemplated, or which the President was authorized to accept, was the regiment, and that, beyond the power of the Confederate Government to arm the volunteers, they were required to be armed by the States from which they came. The law treated the possession of arms as the condition on which volunteers might be accepted, but the English Adjutant-General, in haste to censure, does not stop to inquire whether his "men in buckram" *had* arms.

Again, a military critic should know that, although arms are indispensable, munitions of war are also absolutely essential to troops in campaign; and his knowledge need not be very profound to lead him to the conclusion that ammunition was necessary to make guns effective. Of the early and active efforts made to obtain military supplies notice will be taken in the progress of this article.

There is not a shadow of a shade of truth in Lord Wolseley's statement that I began my duties as President of the Confederacy with "the avowed expectation that 10,000 Enfield rifles would be sufficient to overawe the United States." It is a fact of ineffaceable record that I publicly and always predicted a long and bloody struggle, and for that reason was often criticised and censured by the more ardent advocates of secession and termed "slow" and "too conservative." No Southern man had enjoyed better opportunities than my public life in Washington had given me to gauge the resources and predict the probable policy of the people of the North; for, as Senator, I had long and intimately associated with their representatives, and for four years had been United States Secretary of War. With such opportunities of ascertaining the power and sentiments of the Northern people, it would have shown an inexcusable want of perception if I had shared the hopes of men less favored with opportunities for forming correct judgments, in believing with them that secession could be or would be peacefully accomplished.

The absurdity of these statements may further be seen from the fact that, as appears from the official report of General Gorgas,* chief of ordnance of the Confederacy both under the provisional and the permanent government, there was in the armories of the Confederate States, subject to my order as Commander-in-Chief, a supply of arms, inadequate, indeed, for the needs of the country, but vastly in excess of the number that, according to my military-imaginative critic, I had declared sufficient to overawe the United States; and yet it is of public record that, even before I had selected the members of the provisional cabinet, or engaged a private secretary, or had any clerical assistance whatever, one of my first acts as Provisional President, at Montgomery, was to commission Captain (afterwards Admiral) Raphael Semmes to proceed north and purchase all the arms, ammunition, and other munitions of war, and the machinery for making them, that he could buy and have delivered. In Admiral Semmes's "Memoirs of Service Afloat," it will be found on page 82 and the following pages that he reached Montgomery on the 19th of February, 1861, the day after the inauguration of President Davis. He there states that he called upon the President, who conversed with him on the want of preparation for defence and asked Captain Semmes if he could make use of him, and explained his purpose to send him to the Northern States to gather together, with as much haste as possible, mechanics skilled in the manufacture and use of ordnance and rifle machinery, the preparation of fixed ammunition, percussion caps, etc. "He had not selected all his cabinet, nor, indeed, had he so much as a private secretary at his command, as the letter of instructions which he presented for my guidance was written with his own hand. This letter was very full and precise, frequently descending into detail and manifesting an acquaintance with bureau duties scarcely to have been expected," etc.

Subsequently, upon the appointment of Mr. Mallory as Sec-

* General Gorgas reports that at the formation of the government the small arms at command were 15,000 rifles and 120,000 muskets, stored at Fayetteville, Richmond, Charleston, Augusta, Mount Vernon (Ala.), and Baton Rouge. "Besides the foregoing, there were at Little Rock, Ark., a few thousand stands, and some few at the Texas arsenal, increasing the aggregate of serviceable arms to, say, 143,000. To these must be added the arms owned by the several States and by military organizations throughout the country, giving, say, 150,000 in all for the use of the armies of the Confederacy." That is, *fifteen-fold* more than, according to Lord Wolseley, I had "avowed" as necessary to "overawe" the United States. So earnest were the efforts made by the Confederate Government to increase this number of effective arms that the chief-of-ordnance report of July 1, 1863, shows that there was then a total of infantry arms, acquired from all sources, of 400,000.

retary of the Navy, he sent, March 13, 1861, a letter further instructing Captain Semmes to look out for any vessels suited for coast defence; and Captain Semmes writes: "Under these instructions I made diligent search in the waters of New York for such steamers as were wanted, but none could be found." Admiral Semmes adds:

"I found the people everywhere not only willing, but anxious, to contract with me. I purchased large quantities of percussion caps in the city of New York, and sent them by express without any disguise to Montgomery. I made contracts for batteries of light artillery, powder, and other munitions, and succeeded in getting large quantities of the powder shipped. I made a contract for removal to the Southern States of a complete set of machinery for rifling cannon, with the requisite skilled workmen to put it in operation."

The interference of the civil authorities prevented many of these contracts from being fulfilled at a later date.

General Gorgas, chief of ordnance, writes:

"As to a further supply of arms, steps had been taken by the President to import these and other ordnance stores from Europe, and Major Caleb Huse, graduate of West Point, and at that moment professor in the University of Alabama, was selected to go abroad and procure them. He left Montgomery under instructions from me early in April, 1861, with a credit of £10,000 from Mr. Memminger. The appointment proved a happy one; for he succeeded, with very little money, in contracting for a good supply and in running my department in debt for nearly half a million—the very best proof of his fitness for his place and of a financial ability which supplemented the narrowness of Mr. Memminger's purse."

II.—"*The man who neglected to buy the East Indian fleet, which happy chance and the zeal of subordinates threw in his way.*"

My first knowledge of the existence of such a story was derived from the New York *Sun* of November 17, 1878, in which appeared what purported to be an interview with General G. T. Beauregard to the effect that he had gone "with the messenger of Messrs. Frazer & Co. to Montgomery, had introduced the messenger to the Secretary of War, and took advantage of the opportunity to urge upon him the immediate adoption of the proposition, which was to buy some six large and strong steamers just built in England for the East India Company." I thereupon wrote to General L. P. Walker, ex-Secretary of War of the Confederate States, sending him the New York *Sun* and requesting such information as he might have in regard to the matter, and I received the following reply:

HUNTSVILLE, Ala., December 10, 1878.
Hon. JEFFERSON DAVIS, Beauvoir, Miss.

DEAR SIR: I have read the article in the New York *Sun*, which you enclosed in your letter to me of the 2d inst. I do not remember the interview with me mentioned by General Beauregard, nor that any proposition was submitted to the Confederate Government for the sale to it of any steamers of the character stated here. If any such proposition was made, it has passed from my recollection.

Yours respectfully,

L. P. WALKER.

To a like inquiry addressed to Mr. Memminger, ex-Secretary of the Confederate Treasury, he replied, on November 27, 1878:

CHARLESTON, S. C,, November 27, 1878.

Hon. JEFF DAVIS, Beauvoir, Miss.

MY DEAR SIR: I have no recollection of having heard of the proposition referred to by General Beauregard. I remember my having written to Mr. Trenholm, one of the firm of Jno. Frazer & Co., to come on to Montgomery to present the advantages of establishing a depot for cotton and munitions of war at Bermuda and some station in the West Indies, and that he came on and appeared before the Cabinet, and warmly advocated this plan, and that it met with my cordial approval, but it was not approved by the Cabinet.

I remember nothing of any proposal to purchase the steamers of the India Company. Mr. William Trenholm remembers his appearance before the Cabinet in behalf of the scheme above mentioned. His address was confined to that scheme, but he says he made the proposition to the Secretary of War and to Mr. Mallory, the Secretary of the Navy, to purchase the steamers of the Oriental Company, but that they had many grounds of objection to the purchase, such as the great draught of water, which would prevent their entering Southern ports,their construction of iron, and the want of money. He has no recollection of ever having spoken to me or you on the subject, nor did it enter into the statement made before the Cabinet; and as to myself, I have no recollection of having been consulted by either Mr. Mallory or the Secretary of the War.

Very truly yours,

C. G. MEMMINGER.

It would be needless to consider why I "refused" a proposition which was never made to me, and I can only remand both the refusal and the reason for it to the region of imagination from which they sprang.

The Confederate States, being without ship-yards and without skilled workmen with whom to build cruisers and to provide for coast defences, were compelled to look abroad both to buy and to build the vessels they required. Capt. J. D. Bullock, a well-known officer of the United States Navy, had, immediately after his resignation, reported at Montgomery for orders, and was selected to go abroad as our chief naval agent in Europe. He left Montgomery on May 9, 1861, to get cruising ships of suitable type afloat with the quickest possible despatch and to buy and forward naval supplies of all kinds without delay. Whoever has read his work, entitled "Secret Service of the Confederate States in Europe," will not fail to perceive how fortunate was the selection for the vitally important duty on which he was sent abroad. The diligence and energy with which he filled the office intrusted to him are attested by the list of ships built and bought by him in Europe by the Confederate States Navy Department, viz., five steam cruisers, one sailing vessel, eight steam blockade-runners, one steamer for harbor defence, four steamers contracted for, but unfinished at the close of the war; total, fifteen furnished and four under construction. Nor was this all which was contributed; for, meagre as the means were from the beginning to the end of the war, there were continuous efforts to create and utilize all existing means for defence. To the Confederacy the world is indebted for the introduction of iron-clad ships. A vessel abandoned by the United States was shielded with railroad iron for the want of plates, and made a record at Hampton Roads which can never be forgotten.

I have just received (August 13) a letter from Captain Bullock, containing important testimony. Captain Bullock, as stated above, was appointed by me, when Provisional President, as the sole agent of the Confederate States in Europe for the purchase of arms, cruisers, transports, and naval munitions of war. He was appointed a captain of the Confederate States as soon as he resigned his commission in the United States Navy. His letter is as follows:

30 SYDENHAM AVENUE, SIFTON PARK, LIVERPOOL, July 29, 1889.

MY DEAR SIR: Mr. Stoess handed me your letter of the 15th instant this morning, and I hasten to reply by the first returning steamer. I have never seen the book to which you allude, namely, "The Military Operations of General G. T. Beauregard,' but, in June, 1884, Mr. Charles K. Prioleau, who was then living in Bruges, sent me a copy of the Charleston *News and Courier* which contained a long, interesting, and very able review of the work.

The reviewer gave many extracts from the book, and among them one stating, in effect, that a fleet of steamers belonging to the East Indian Navy had been offered to the Confederate Government at the beginning of the war, and had been declined by them, and that the offer had been made by or through Mr. Charles K. Prioleau. Mr. Prioleau was the senior partner of the Liverpool firm of Fraser, Trenholm & Co., a firm affiliated with Messrs. John Fraser & Co., of Charleston, and the Liverpool branch held the position of the bankers and financial agents of the Confederate Government during the war of secession. Mr. Prioleau was then brought into close personal and official relations with me during the whole period of that war, and as he had never mentioned to me this alleged offer to the Confederate Government, nor had ever drawn my attention to any such ships, I was greatly surprised by the statement in the review of "General Beauregard's Military Operations." I wrote at once to Mr. Prioleau, asking him for information and requesting him, if there was any truth in the statement, to tell me why he never mentioned the matter to me. He wrote me a very long letter in reply, much of its contents being wholly irrelevant to the point at issue, but I enclose herewith a paper marked A*, which is a verbatim copy of all that he wrote in respect to my specific inquiries about the alleged offer to the Confederate Government.

When I went to Richmond in October, 1861, to consult with Mr. Mallory about our naval operations in Europe, he dwelt much upon the wish of the government to get cruisers afloat, and also armored ships to break the blockade. It is not possible to believe that he would have omitted all allusion to the East Indian Company's fleet, if he had ever heard of those vessels. I had just then returned from England with the "Fingal," and, as before mentioned, Mr. Prioleau had given me not a hint of the alleged offer. After my return to Europe, I both heard of and saw some of the ships, but a glance satisfied me that to buy them for the Confederate Navy would have been a senseless waste of money. They were very big ships, drawing too much water to enter any Confederate port on the Atlantic coast. At the time I saw them they were wholly dismantled, and without guns or any military equipment. To arm and man them for the purpose of attacking the blockading ships would have required the resources of a well-furnished dock-yard, and the right to enlist seamen without interference. It would have been impossible to equip so large a naval force upon the high seas, or at some secret place of rendezvous, as was done with the "Alabama" and other cruisers. To put those ten ships in fighting condition would have required about one hundred heavy guns, and from twelve to fifteen hundred seamen, stokers, etc., with a large supply of small arms and ordnance stores. It would also have been necessary to have several large coal-transports to accompany the fleet, as the ships had only auxiliary sail power, and were dependent upon steam for motive power.

If Mr. Mallory had ever suggested the purchase of these ships, I should just have mentioned the foregoing facts, and have drawn his attention to the proclamation of Her Britannic Majesty, the British neutrality laws, and the restrictions in respect to

* A.

BRUGES, 21st June, 1884.

MY DEAR BULLOCK:

. . . As regards the ten steamers, I thought you knew about them. They were a part of the East India Company's fleet, the "Golden Fleece," "Jason," "Hydaspes," etc.; they were offered to me at the very beginning of the war, before you came over, and before the Queen's proclamation. My idea was that if they could have been armed and got out, they would have swept away every vestige of a Federal blockader then upon the water. Fraser, Trenholm & Co. had not then been appointed agents of the government, and I did not offer these vessels to the government, but I mentioned them in a private letter to Mr. G. A. Trenholm, leaving it to his discretion to put it before them.

As a matter of fact, I never got any reply to this letter and never knew that the ships had even been proposed to the government till long after the war. No further inquiries were ever made of me concerning them from any quarter. About nine or ten years (or perhaps not quite so much) ago, General Beauregard wrote me, saying that he was engaged upon his history, that he had heard about these steamers through William Trenholm, who had referred him to me for the particulars, and asked me if I would give him a statement, and allow him to mention my name as to my part of the transaction, to which I willingly consented and gave him just the facts stated above. Of course, I know *now* that the enterprise would have been impossible, but we did not know anything for certain then; and any opinion of mine would have been that of a layman and on its face valueless; therefore, when I heard no more I naturally concluded either that Mr. Trenholm had not thought it worth while to propose the undertaking, or that the government had been advised against it by their competent officers, and there is no doubt now that they were quite right not to risk so large a sum of money on so doubtful an enterprise, even if they could have readily raised it. It is, however, a little strange that, if the government knew of these ships at the time you left, they did not instruct you to look at them. On the whole, I am inclined to think that they were never offered to the government at all, but William Trenholm knew of them from having access to his father's correspondence. . . .

I am, ever yours sincerely,

C. K. PRIOLEAU.

the coaling of belligerent ships proclaimed by all the neutral powers, and he would have perceived the impracticability of such an undertaking. At a later period of the war Mr. Mallory did direct me to examine two vessels, which I have reason to believe belonged to the same fleet. On page 253, Vol. II., of "The Secret Service of the Confederate States," you will find my report with reference to them. I think at the moment of nothing else worth mentioning on the subject of your letter, but will be glad to give you any further information you may wish, if in my power to do so.

Very faithfully yours,
JAMES D. BULLOCK.

To Hon. JEFFERSON DAVIS.

In the face of facts like these, and many others to which the want of space does not permit me to refer, this self-constituted authority upon military affairs and civil government, ignorantly or maliciously—to me it matters not which—proceeds on an assumption which had no real foundation to characterize me as

III.—*" The ruler who could not see that the one vital necessity for the South was, at all sacrifice and at all hazard, to keep the ports open."*

An Englishman of ordinary intelligence might be expected to know how vigilant his government was in preventing even unarmed merchantmen from leaving their ports, if any one would allege that they were intended to be converted into war-ships for the use of the Confederate States. The espionage to which Captain Bullock was subjected and the delays which resulted from forcing him to appeal to the courts must show how flippant and absurd it is to assert that a fleet of steamers might have been purchased, manned, and equipped, and sent out as cruisers to raise the blockade of Confederate ports. Captain Bullock, vigilant and active, inquiring as well in the ports of Great Britain as those of the Continent, seems never to have found this fleet of steamers so admirably adopted to war purposes that with them the Gulf and Atlantic seaboard might have been so cleanly swept that the commander of the fleet should have carried a broom at his masthead.

The next arraignment by Lord Wolseley's unbridled imagination is to describe me as

IV.—*" The ruler who rejected all means proposed by others for placing the finances of the Confederacy on a sound basis."*

This is understood to be the long-ago-exploded theory that the Confederacy should have sent out the cotton crop of 1860-'61 and placed it as the basis of credit in Europe. In answer to this visionary charge against the administration as the cause of Confederate failure, Mr. C. G. Memminger, the Secretary of the Treasury, on the 27th of March, 1874, wrote to the editor of the Charleston *News and Courier* a letter from which the following conclusive extracts are made :

"The Confederate Government was organized in February, 1861. The blockade was instituted in May, thus leaving a period of three months in which the whole cotton crop on hand, say 4,000,000 bales, ought, according to this military financier, to have been got into the hands of the Confederate Government and to have been shipped abroad. This would have required a fleet of four thousand ships, allowing one thousand bales to the ship! Where would these vessels have been procured in the face of the notification of the blockade? and was not as much of the cotton shipped by private enterprise as could have been shipped by the government? When so shipped, the proceeds of the sale were in most cases sold to the government in the shape of bills of exchange. The superior advantage of this plan is evinced by the fact that throughout the year the government exchanged its own notes for bills on England at par, with which it paid for all its arms and munitions of war. . . .

"C. G. MEMMINGER."

In answer to the same vague assertion, G. A. Trenholm, the successor of Mr. Memminger in the Treasury Department, wrote to the editor of the Charleston *News and Courier* a full answer, from which I make the following extract :

"Let us examine the facts upon which this theory rests, and without the support of which it must necessarily fall to the ground. The crop of cotton available for this scheme must have been that of 1860-'61. It could not have been the crop of which the seed was not yet put in the ground when the government was formed at Montgomery. What was, then, the crop of 1860-'61? Was it 4,000,000 to 5,000,000 bales, and was it accessible for immediate exportation? . . . Up to the 28th of February, the month that gave birth to the infant government, 3,000,000 bales had been received at the seaports, and the great bulk of it had been exported to Europe, or been sold to the New England spinners. By the 1st of May 586,000 bales more had been received and sold. England and the Continent took 3,127,000 bales; the New England spinners 654,000 bales. It will thus be seen that before the new government was fairly organized *the entire crop was already beyond its reach!* Another crop followed, but the exportation in any quantity was an absolute impossibility. There were no vessels in the ports of the Confederacy. The last had left before the expiration of the sixty days allowed to foreign tonnage. The only vessels that took cotton after that time were the foreign steamers that ran the blockade to procure cargoes for the owners. They came in small numbers, and one or two at a time. Had the government seized one of them for its own use or prevented them from leaving with cotton, they would have ceased to come.'

These extracts from the letters of two of the ablest financiers of the South, whose close relation to the Treasury Department gave them the best opportunity of knowing what could, should, or might have been done, will, it is hoped, be satisfactory to any who have doubted the propriety of the financial policy of the Confederacy, or who have not seen that the plan proposed was utterly impracticable.

JEFFERSON DAVIS.

AN ENGLISH VIEW OF THE CIVIL WAR.

BY THE RIGHT HON. VISCOUNT WOLSELEY, ADJUTANT-GENERAL OF THE BRITISH ARMY.

THE *Century* Company has, in my judgment, done a great service to the soldiers of all armies by the publication of these records of the great War* in the United States. The first volume of the republication has just reached me, and I propose in the following pages to restrict my comments to that part of the history embraced within the seven hundred-odd pages it contains.

The story of the War, as told by the several actors in it, has not, in this volume, reached the date at which I personally paid a visit to one of the contending armies. I can only, therefore, comment on the evidence supplied to us, as a deeply interested student of the mighty struggle. The characteristic features of this part of the history are very unlike those of the later campaigns. The attention of soldiers in Europe has been so much directed to the long series of campaigns that were fought over the ground between Washington and Richmond, that we are prone to regard them as representing the character of the War throughout. The elaborately-prepared defensive positions of the later campaigns, and the sharp counter-strokes with which Lee, using Stonewall Jackson as his right arm, met the continued and systematic process of attrition applied by the Northern generals, have hardly their counterpart in this earlier period of the War. Nor do those far-reaching raids of mounted men on either side, which afterwards gave such a distinctive character to the War, appear to have yet made themselves felt.

The stately figure of Robert Lee, as yet, remains in the background. It is, however, excessively interesting to get clearer views than we have hitherto had of the circumstances under which Grant, Sherman, Sheridan, Jackson, and others first made their appearance in this great struggle. The story of the first battle of Bull Run, and of Shiloh, are each told here with much cir-

---

* "Battles and Leaders of the Civil War" (The *Century* War Book).

cumstantial detail that supplies most valuable corrections to what we knew of them before. The stories of the capture of Fort Henry and of Fort Donelson have a very different aspect, now that we are able to judge of them from both sides and from many points of view. To English soldiers, all the minor circumstances of the gathering of the Northern and Southern forces have a special interest, as they enable us to realize in a new way the analagous incidents which must have attended the beginning of the war between King and Parliament in Charles I.'s time. The uncertainty as to which side men would take, the acts of vigorous, personal individuality, like those of Captain Lyon in Missouri, were common to both epochs. The trains with recruits for both sides, passing one another almost amicably on the same American railroad, with other kindred incidents, are all just of such a kind as must have happened in England, when men rallied to the standards of Rupert and of Cromwell. In the later instance, however, they were strangely affected in their form by all the elaborations of modern civilization and by the vastness of the theatre of war,—an area in which our whole island would be lost.

It is with the deepest regret that I feel obliged, at this early part of my review of the War, to call in question the fitness of Mr. Jefferson Davis for the high position he occupied. A man weighed down with years, with misfortunes, and, above all, with sad memories of a lost cause, and, I presume, the conviction that he was a failure, appeals to our pity rather than invites our censure. Like all the great actors on both sides, he was, I am sure, influenced in the course he took by the highest motives. He sincerely believed in the justice of the cause he espoused, and he brought to the service of his country an honesty of purpose, a fervid patriotism, an ability of no mean order, a zeal, and a persistent determination which all will admit he possessed. But that he was a third-rate man, and a most unfortunate selection for the office of President, I cannot conceal from myself. The great misfortunes of public servants who have utterly failed in the one great public venture of their lives must not be allowed to silence the voice of censure, much less of criticism. In dealing with private individuals we can afford to indulge our amiable feelings for misfortune. What we owe to historical truth and to the teaching of future generations forbids us, however, to deal similarly with men who have filled high positions. I note it here as a curious and, in my opinion, a regrettable fact, that in this, the first volume of "Battles and Leaders of the Civil War," there is no picture of the President of the Confederate States, although there are likenesses of many much less important men on both sides in this great struggle. The tremendous indictment against his capacity, which is drawn by Mr. R. Barnwell Rhett, so strongly supports my views regarding him that I regret very much that no answer to it has been printed side by side with it, in accordance with the impartial method of "The *Century* War Series." What reasonable answer could be made to it? If the Northern troops had then really known how he unwittingly worked for them, would they have wished to "hang Jeff. Davis to a sour-apple tree"?

It may be said that it was impossible for any one to foresee the dimensions to which the struggle would grow. But surely it is a statesman's business at least partially to gauge the strength of the forces with which he has to deal. The *soi-disant* statesman who began his high duties with the avowed expectation that 10,000 Enfield rifles would be sufficient to overawe the United States; who then refused the services of 366,000 men, the flower of the South, and accepted only a fraction of them, because he had not arms for more; the man who neglected to buy the East Indian fleet, which happy chance and the zeal of subordinates threw in his way; the ruler who could not see that the one vital necessity for the South was, at all sacrifice and at all hazard, to keep the ports open; who rejected all means proposed by others for placing the finances of the Confederacy on a sound basis,—that man, as I think, did more than any other individual on either side to save the Union. I have not attempted to make the charge against him as complete and crushing as it could easily be made by those who trusted him with almost unlimited powers in their behalf. Enough has been said to illustrate what, I think, is, on this point, the commonly accepted verdict of history.

It is the old, old story over again, of civil rulers who blunder, and, failing to foresee events, sacrifice everything to a momentary popularity, in order to divert popular wrath from themselves to the unfortunate soldiers who have been their victims. An illustration of my meaning is to be found in the pathetic story told in this volume of the gallant and high-minded Albert Sidney Johnston. Like Robert Lee, he hated the War, and had also refused the highest military position in the United States Army, at the call of what he considered to be his duty to his State. Those who played the part of statesmen on the Southern side had left Johnston without resources. Despite all his efforts, and despite his zeal and great military ability, he was overwhelmed by the popular fury at a failure for which others had prepared the way, and where the action of his Government had rendered success well-nigh impossible. To do Mr. Davis justice, he no doubt, in this instance, did his best to support by words the soldier whom he had failed to support by deeds.

To pass to other matters: I am struck, throughout the whole story of the minor operations of this period, by the illustrations they afford of the regularity with which the old rules and principles of war assert their supremacy. The battle of Wilson's Creek, on August 10, 1861, and that of Pea Ridge, on March 7, 1862, are curiously alike in their military lessons. In both, the attempt was made to carry out distinctly separated movements by isolated parts of an attacking force, in order to strike upon the flanks or rear of a concentrated defensive force. Both attempts failed, as might have been predicted beforehand. No doubt Sigel's movement round the rear of Price at Wilson's Creek was a more hazardous, as well as a bolder, attempt than that of Price and McCulloch at Pea Ridge, so far as their separation on the field of battle was concerned. But McCulloch, at Pea Ridge, was completely disconnected from the attack made upon the Federal right by Price. The consequences in each battle followed in the same way. McCulloch, at Pea Ridge, and Sigel, at Wilson's Creek, each for the moment gained advantage from a surprised enemy; but when time had been given for the surprised to recover, there was in neither instance a supporting force sufficiently near at hand to meet the supports brought up by the enemy. The advantage gained at first was soon lost, and then the isolated force was crushed. The result was, in each instance, that the depending army was thus soon able to devote its whole strength to meet the remainder of the attack, and to crush that in its turn also. It is worthy of note that, in the general position taken up for the attack, Price had passed completely to the rear of the Federal position. It is clear that he sacrificed as much as he gained by so doing. The Federals were as directly on his line of communications as he on theirs.

I am much struck, in this intricate series of minor actions, by the terrible difficulty under which generals act who are in command of troops that cannot be employed solely to win victory, and to bring about peace by securing it. I refer to the necessity which the leaders on both sides had to yield to, of retaining often large forces for the defence of points of political, but of small military, importance, if of any at all. McCulloch, tied to the defence of the trans-Mississippi region, and especially to that of Arkansas, on the Indian territory, could not, perhaps would not, join with Price in any large military movement. Here, as always, the orders from the Civil Government at Richmond hampered the military movement of the Confederate leaders; otherwise it is clear that a far more effective mode of meeting the Federal advance could have been devised than that of passing round to their rear. The Federal forces, based on St. Louis, had advanced by way of Rolla, Lebanon, and Dug Spring to the Pea Ridge. (See map on page 263.) Van Dorn had his headquarters at Pocahontas. Price had fallen back before the Federal Army as it advanced. McCulloch was, at first, at Maysville. It is not very clear from any of the narratives how much force Van Dorn, who was in command of the whole, had gathered at Pocahontas; but, as he had been contemplating a movement on St. Louis, he must, at least, have collected a considerable quantity of stores at Pocahontas. It would seem that McCulloch might have been at once transferred to the eastern side of the White River, allowing Price to continue his retreat towards the same point. General Curtis, when he reached Pea Ridge with the Federal force, entered a most difficult country; and had Price gradually given him the slip, with a view to a junction with the other Confederate forces, it is clear that an advance northward, directly upon Rolla or Springfield, based on Pocahontas, would have obliged Curtis to abandon his invasion of Arkansas, and would have enabled Van Dorn to fight at far greater advantage than he actually did. The Federal line, even from Rolla to Sugar Creek, was two hundred and ten miles in length, and from St. Louis it was three hundred and twenty miles. It would have been exposed throughout that entire distance to such a stroke from Pocahontas.

I do not, however, say this as a criticism on the generals on either side. No one who has himself realized the practical difficulties of command in the field is much tempted to any slap-dash criticism of those who are engaged in high command. The lesson which is most impressed upon me by a study of these campaigns is the danger there always is of popular irritability and ignorant impatience preventing a general from doing the very thing which would, if time were allowed, surely gain the ends which the people desire. If England were invaded, or threatened with invasion, the general in supreme command would be exposed to the same difficulty. People in Manchester would be uneasy because the Lancashire Volunteer Corps were drawn away from the defence of their own locality, for the purpose of crushing the enemy in the field elsewhere, by the united action of all our available military forces. It is for this reason that I hope the *Century's* admirable narrative of the Confederate War may be read attentively by the large numbers of educated volunteer officers whom we now have in England. Its campaigns are replete with instruction for all our auxiliary forces, as well as for our army.

In 1866, during the western campaign in Germany, very similar events repeated themselves. There, Vogel von Falkenstein, with a numerically very inferior force of Prussians, triumphed over the army opposed to him—an army made up of Hanoverians, Wurtembergers, Bavarians, and troops of various other minor states—because the officers commanding each contingent were hampered by their respective civil governments with orders which had their origin in a desire to keep each its own troops for the defence of its own particular state. Hence the absence of all unity of action, and the impossibility of concentration upon the decisive points. On the other hand, the Prussians triumphed because they were everywhere directed upon the decisive points against enemies whose several interests kept them from working heartily together. I dwell upon this because I have heard English politicians say that, in the event of danger here, we should have great difficulties with localities, which would cry out against having their volunteer corps removed for the defence of distant, though possibly most vital, points.

This great principle of strategy rules everywhere; and although I have every wish to do justice to the ability of General Albert Sidney Johnston, it is impossible to accept the reasons which his son advances for his having allowed General Curtis to attack Fort Donelson without moving to resist him, when he was, himself, within supporting distance at Nashville. The statement that he was bound to remain at Nashville, because it was the objective point of the Federal campaign, is answered by the facts. He was immediately obliged to abandon Nashville and to fall back on Corinth, as soon as Donelson fell. As long as the point of Federal attack was uncertain, it would seem to have been quite permissible for him to divide his forces between Donelson and Nashville, each of which was of great importance. What appears to me certain is that the course which was pursued by the Confederate commanders, prior to the first Bull Run, would here have been the right one. Whilst Buell's advance on Nashville was delayed, and Grant's attack on Donelson was declared, it would have been well to demonstrate in advance of Nashville, so as to convey the impression of intended aggression from that point, just as in the early summer of 1861 General Joseph E. Johnston did against Patterson, before he moved to support Beauregard, then in position on Bull Run.

If a similar course had been followed in Kentucky and Tennessee in February, 1862, and a rapid movement made with all the troops which General Albert S. Johnston could have then collected to attack Grant before Fort Donelson, it is difficult to believe, considering what actually did happen there, that the Federal forces could have escaped decisive defeat. It is evident that the personal presence of General A. S. Johnston himself was badly needed at Fort Donelson, and the moral effect of his arrival there with fresh troops would have been enormous. Such a success would have greatly assisted Van Dorn's campaign, and if that campaign had been conducted in the way suggested, on the line from Pocahontas towards Rolla, the forces under Johnston and Van Dorn would have occupied a central position between Buell and Curtis, and might have struck with great advantage at either. That such a coöperation between Van Dorn and A. S. Johnston was not rendered impossible by any material obstacles, or by distance, is clear from the fact that, previous to Shiloh, Beauregard was looking for support from Van Dorn (page 574) on February 21, three days before Van Dorn started for the Pea Ridge campaign, and whilst Van Dorn was still at Pocahontas.

I shall not enter into the disputed claims of General Beauregard and of General A. S. Johnson to have conceived the scheme of the Shiloh campaign. Whoever conceived it, the advance to attack Grant where he stood in position was in every respect a sound military operation.

It is curious to see how differently men regard operations in which they have been personally engaged and those in which they have had no special or direct interest. General Grant's own account of Shiloh leaves one the impression that he is conscious that his proceedings there were not militarily defensible. I hardly know of two commanders to whose sound military judgment I would more unhesitatingly commit the following proposition than Generals Grant and Sherman, supposing it were possible to do so, and that it could be put to them regarding an action in which they had not been personally concerned. I cannot do better than state the proposition in the terms, and in what seems to me the unanswerable criticism, of General Buell, given on page 487.

"An army comprising seventy regiments of infantry, twenty batteries of artillery, and a sufficiency of cavalry, lay for two weeks and more in isolated camps, with a river in its rear, and a hostile army, claimed to be superior in numbers, twenty miles distant in its front, while the commander made his headquarters and passed his nights nine miles away on the opposite side of the river. It had no line or order of battle, no defensive works of any sort, no outposts, properly speaking, to give warning, or check the advance of an enemy and no recognized head during the absence of the regular commander. On a Saturday the hostile force arrived and formed in order of battle, without detection or hindrance, within a mile and a half of the unguarded army, advanced upon it the next morning, penetrated its disconnected lines, assaulted its camps in front and flank, drove its disjointed members successively from position to position, capturing some and routing others, in spite of much heroic resistance, and steadily drew near the landing and depot of its supplies in the pocket between the river and an impassable creek."

Had not the commander of that assailed army positively invited defeat? Is there a syllable in that summary of the facts which does not accurately represent the incidents of the first day's fight at Shiloh?

It is hoped that no one will imagine for a moment that I wish to throw a stone at General Grant. We are all of us liable to human error. The greatest generals have made great, perhaps some of the greatest, mistakes ever made in war. The matter is looked at solely as a question of military study, and, looking so, it would not appear that General Buell's criticism, in the chapter called "Shiloh Reviewed," admits of any good answer. No satisfactory answer is, in my opinion, supplied to it by General Grant's statements on the battle of Shiloh. As a matter of fact, it would seem that Grant and Sherman before Shiloh, like Wellington and Blucher before Quatre Bras and Ligny, were contemplating an offensive, not a defensive, campaign. By coupling together these names as I have done, I shall perhaps best show that I am not speaking with any disparagement of Grant or of Sherman.

In both instances alike, the error of taking for granted that an active and able enemy is restricted to one course of action, was severely punished. In both cases alike, it very narrowly missed being fatally punished. In no other way, with, perhaps, the reservation that Grant had not at that time acquired the experience he afterwards gained, can I explain the facts. Grant was avowedly waiting for the arrival of Buell's force to begin an offensive campaign with a united army. By means of his gunboats he had complete command of the passage of the Tennessee. Supposing that it was advisable to make the concentration in the neighborhood of Pittsburg Landing, clearly the right course would have been to cover that concentration by the river, and, therefore, to have retained the bulk of his forces concentrated on the east bank, awaiting Buell's arrival. If it were necessary, as perhaps it was, to secure Pittsburg Landing itself, as a means of debouching on the opposite bank, there could have been no objection, and probably would have been advantage, in having a small, strongly-intrenched position near that point, in the nature of a bridge-head, with its flanks thoroughly swept by the fire of the gunboats. Clearly, if, as General Grant says, the troops required discipline and drill more than work at intrenchments, it would have been easier and safer to impart both to them on the east bank of the river, away from the enemy, than on the west bank within his easy reach.

The accidents and mistakes which occurred in regard to the march of General Wallace's division were only such as continually occur when a change in the position of troops, that has not been previously arranged for and worked out beforehand, is suddenly ordered in any sudden exigency. As an admirable illustration of the kind of method that makes all the difference between success and failure in war, the student should carefully compare the arrangements made for the march of General Lew Wallace's division with the—on the surface—apparently very similar steps taken by Napoleon before Austerlitz, for the due arrival of Davoust's corps. Napoleon deliberately kept that corps away from Austerlitz till the actual day of battle, in a way that might, to a careless student, seem similar to that which left General Lew Wallace within a march of the field of Shiloh. The difference lay in this: Napoleon had been for weeks watching closely the movements of the Allies, and had been endeavoring to tempt them to attack him, by not allowing the forces that he knew he could count on for the field of battle to be apparently within reach. Every detail for Davoust's march had been carefully thought out and prepared beforehand. He was destined to arrive on a part of the field where it was important to encourage the enemy to attack, where the enemy's advance must necessarily be slow, and where it was advisable to allow him to secure some temporary advantage. All this had been previously designed.

On the other hand, for days before Shiloh nothing was known of the movements of Johnston and Beauregard. No attack from them was either expected or prepared for. The direction of Lew Wallace's march depended on his correctly interpreting a single loosely-worded order. The very position of his three brigades seems to have been imperfectly known at Grant's headquarters, for the order of march was certainly not made in accordance with their actual position. Time and distance are elements of vital importance in all these matters. Altogether, the more one studies this first day's battle on the Federal side, the more clear it seems that the opportunity presented to the enemy for attack was as favorable as it well could have been. It is hardly necessary to insist upon the point so well made by General Buell in the passage I have quoted, that the risk was enormously enhanced by the fact that this detached and isolated army, unprepared as it was to resist attack, was liable to be driven "into the pocket between the river," which it had so rashly crossed, and an "impassable creek." When the opportunity is presented to a commander for an attack upon any fraction of a hostile army then in the act of concentrating against him, there are two conditions for which he prays. One is that there shall be time and opportunity for defeating the fraction in question before it can be supported. The other is that the position of the fraction shall be such that, when once defeated, it shall be so utterly broken up and demolished that it can render no assistance to the new supporting force which may possibly arrive.

Both these conditions were presented to Generals Beauregard and Johnston when they designed the march to attack Grant at Shiloh. Seeing the enormous change in the whole situation which would have been wrought if the first day's action had been final and conclusive, it is of great interest to consider, from the

Confederate side, what the circumstances were which deprived them of the success which seemed so nearly within their grasp.

It seems tolerably clear that, had everything been done as rapidly as it might have been, the Confederates could and would have made their attack on Saturday, April 5, instead of on Sunday, April 6, 1862. If the attack had been thus made twenty-four hours earlier than it was, I think nothing could have saved Grant's army from complete destruction. Buell had pressed his march, despite the fact that Grant had not proposed to send boats to Savannah "till Monday or Tuesday, or some time early in the week," and had always written in the sense of his words on that very Saturday in Nelson's camp: "There will be no fighting at Pittsburg Landing; we will have to go to Corinth, where the rebels are fortified. If they come to attack us, we can whip them, as I have more than twice as many troops as I had at Fort Donelson." Considering the state of the rivers and bridges, as described by Buell, it seems impossible that any portion of his force should have arrived earlier than it did. Nothing would have tended to change the conditions of Lew Wallace's march, and, therefore, as far as one can judge, in all probability Saturday would have placed the Confederates in a position even more favorable than they actually were in by Sunday evening; more favorable because on Saturday their final movement would not have been checked by the arrival of Nelson's division.

In all probability, therefore, even on Saturday evening a final attack would have resulted in the capture of Pittsburg Landing itself, and of the powerful force of reserve artillery concentrated there. In any case, that would have happened on Sunday morning; and, as an incident of the fighting on that day, Lew Wallace, committed, as he would have been, to a position on the Confederate side of Snake Creek, would have been cut off from the only bridge by which he could have returned. Attacked, as he certainly would have been, by overwhelming forces in front, flank, and rear, he must have lost his whole division in a few hours. The Confederates, fully aware of the proximate advance of Buell, would, in that case, have had the greater part of Sunday in which to prepare for him. If Buell had attempted, under these circumstances, to attack, he would have done so under the greatest disadvantages. The whole artillery and all the stores of Grant's army would have been available for employment against him. He must have necessarily landed division by division, because apparently there was not river transport available for more than one division at a time. No doubt the gunboats would have afforded him powerful assistance, but even with their aid the enterprise would have been one which few prudent commanders would have risked. In all probability, he would have been obliged to gather his forces on the further side of the Tennessee, whilst the Confederates, supplied with all the arms and stores of which they stood so sorely in need, would have been joined by thousands of recruits whom they would then have been able effectively to arm and equip. No wonder that the battle has been looked upon, on both sides, as the turning event of the Western War.

What, then, was the cause of the Confederate delay, which proved so fatal to them? It has been remarked by able officers on the Confederate side that, while nothing could have been more admirable than the conception of the attack on Shiloh, nothing could have been more miserable in all details than the execution. That, I take it, was the inevitable result of the condition of the army at the time. Military training and organization would be useless and, certainly, very expensively purchased qualities, if it were possible that an army of recruits, gathered together in the way the army at Corinth was, should be able to execute a well-prepared plan with all the celerity and certainty which attend the movements of veteran armies. The difficulties which the want of experience, the want of drill, the want of discipline, and the want of a highly-trained staff entailed on both armies, are insisted on at every stage by those who took part in the operations. It is, however, in the movements of attack conducted through an intricate country, almost without roads and very imperfectly mapped or known, that these defects of an army tell most severely. An army in a defensive position, requiring relatively little movement, does not feel them nearly so severely. It was in his thorough appreciation of these facts that, later on in the war, General Robert Lee showed his masterly power of adapting means to ends. He always used Jackson's seasoned soldiers for those wide-reaching strokes by means of which he sought to compensate for the inferiority of his less handy troops. The newly-raised battalions, whom he could not trust to manœuvre, but who shot fairly enough, he placed in position where their want of military efficiency was not particularly felt, whilst their strength was evident.

Nevertheless, it is very interesting to note the incidents which, in the mere delivery of orders and in the mode in which they were interpreted, tended to cause delay. The "Notes of a Confederate Staff Officer at Shiloh" (pages 594–603) are in this respect most valuable. General Jordan observes, in a note to page 595 : "As I framed this order, I had before me Napoleon's order for the battle of Waterloo, and, in attention to ante-battle details, took those of such soldiers as Napoleon and Soult for models." Now, it is worth noting that, during the Waterloo campaign, Soult on one or two occasions failed Napoleon as a chief of the staff, not in the drawing-up of orders, but in getting them actually delivered and acted on. The whole movement of Napoleon's army on the 15th was seriously hampered because Vandamme's corps did not move in time, owing to his not having received his orders. In the movement on Shiloh, the army was delayed, and the attack was postponed from Saturday to Sunday, largely because General Polk's corps did not march at the appointed time, he thinking it his duty to await written orders. It had, as we learn, been expressly arranged at a meeting between General Beauregard and the three corps commanders that they should march at twelve, noon, on April 3, without waiting for the written orders containing the detail of their respective routes. General Beauregard himself had, when in bed, worked out these routes during the night of April 2–3 "on the backs of telegrams and envelopes." As it was likely to take some time to reduce these plans and orders to shape, it had been arranged, as already stated, that the corps, to avoid delay, should at once advance over that part of the route which was well known and had been explained previously to their commanders by General Beauregard. It was promised that complete instructions in writing should be sent them on the march.

But it is clear that, while General Beauregard and his staff believed that all the corps generals had understood that they were to move off without waiting for further orders, General Polk, whose corps was leading, had not understood this. According to General Jordan's own account (page 595), the written circular order to the corps commanders directed "that each should hold his corps under arms by 6 A.M. on the 3d of April *ready to march,* with one hundred rounds of ammunition," etc. Now, in a conference of several people it is extremely difficult to be sure that anything which has not been reduced to writing has been understood separately by each of them. Men are very apt to think that everybody else understands what they themselves understand. It seems to me, therefore, that as a lesson of staff-work to be deduced from this experience, which is by no means exceptional, the right course in similar cases would be this : A written memorandum, which could have been drawn out in two minutes, should have been noted by each corps commander to this effect:

"Camp —————, 3d April, 1862.

"It is to be understood that the troops will move off at 12 to-day, under the orders of their corps commanders, without waiting for further instructions from headquarters. Full instructions as to the direction and mode of attack will be sent in due course to each corps commander en route."

This is not suggested as a censure on the actual course pursued by the staff on this occasion. It is only by the reiterated experiences of this kind which war supplies that we learn to avoid the possibilities of future error. Nevertheless, this case and that of Soult at Waterloo, which General Jordan has taken as a model, are illustrations for all soldiers of the number of points which ought to engage the attention of a chief of the staff independent of the mere correct drawing-up of orders. War is big with instances of the importance of the links which connect the actual schemes of operations with their practical execution by means of the feet and legs of men. All our accumulated experience of this kind points to the great importance—I may say the necessity—of the presence, at the right hand of the actual commander, of a chief of the staff, who should be the general who is next to him in genius and ability in the army. The most important function of this chief of the staff is to see that the strategic and tactical plans of the commander are practically worked out and properly executed. It is all very well to design a brilliant stroke, such as that on Shiloh ; but if the men do not actually march at the appointed hour, if a corps like Polk's "somehow blocks the line of march," if, for some reason or other, a corps like Bragg's is moved "with inexplicable tardiness," the best-laid schemes "gang oft agley," as Burns has it.

It is impossible, without a more intimate knowledge of all the circumstances, and of the actual condition of the ground at the time, than those who were not there now possess, not to accept as actual fact the statement of General Beauregard that any movement of the three corps toward the field in three separate columns was "an absolute impossibility." (Page 581, note.) I cannot see that Colonel Johnston has in any way upset this statement by the man who, certainly, from all his circumstances, had the best means of knowing the character of the ground. No one would doubt that, had it been possible, it would have been better and more rapid to move by three roads. As the Confederate force scarcely exceeded 40,000 men of all arms, the term "three corps" tends to give rather an exaggerated impression of the crowding that must have taken place on the two bad roads they actually followed.

It is difficult to judge with certainty, and with absolute fairness to all concerned, the conduct of a very complex action of the kind which followed. Nevertheless, I cannot, for instance, agree with General Beauregard that the whole sequence of events shows that, when once in presence of the position, it would have been better for Johnston not to attack. A retreat under such circumstances would have been most demoralizing. All, or almost all, the reasons which General Beauregard advanced at the time for not carrying out the enterprise proved, in fact, to be mistaken. The enemy were *not* "intrenched up to the eyes," as he believed they would be, or intrenched at all. The enemy had *not* been roused by the clumsy recognizance in force made by part of Bragg's corps. To all intents and purposes, the enemy were completely surprised. Nothing shows it more clearly than the contrast between Grant's words at Nelson's camp at Savannah, the previous evening, which I have already quoted, saying that no attack would be made by the enemy, and the letter he wrote to General Buell during the attack (see page 492), in which he states that "the rebel forces," actually numbering 40,000, "are estimated at over 100,000 men."

All that occurred bespoke it the surprise it actually was. The postponement of the attack from Saturday to Sunday clearly deprived the assailants of their best hope of gaining a crushing victory. Seeing, however, how successful the Confederates were on that day, it seems to me that they stood to win more by the attack than by a retreat, which would have brought down on them the united forces of Grant and Buell, untouched and in full power. As General Buell fairly urges, the Confederates, considering the extent to which they had been able to re-arm and re-equip themselves, were actually stronger at the end than they were at the beginning of the first day, whilst the Federals had been materially weakened. Moreover, despite all that General Beauregard has urged, as to the impossibility of carrying, before nightfall, the last foot-hold of the Federal Army at Pittsburg Landing with the forces then actually up, it was, as far as I can judge, a case where the attacking general himself ought to have pushed to the front, gathering all the forces he could from every quarter, for a final attack. It was then a question of "neck or nothing" with him to push home his victory. Arrangements could have been made afterwards for the disposal of the ample supplies of food and ammunition captured in the Federal camps. It seems that all the evidence on both sides, as to the situation of things along the river bank, tends to confirm the evidence supplied on this point by Colonel Lockett, who was present on the spot. "In our front only one single point was showing fight, a hill crowned with artillery"; Bragg with his forces on the spot was confident of victory, when he was stopped by a messenger from Beauregard saying: "The General directs that the pursuit be stopped; the victory is sufficiently complete; it is needless to expose our men to the fire of the gunboats."

That seems to me to indicate exactly the condition of General Beauregard's mind. The shells of the gunboats were, according to all testimony, telling upon the far-distant rear of the Confederate forces. They were producing, however, no effect whatever on the front, and did not in the slightest degree interfere with the carrying-out of the final assault. But that was a condition of things in which, from his position at Shiloh, General Beauregard could do nothing. He was very much debilitated by bad health; he had not wished that the attack should be made that day at all; he was occupied with the by no means important fighting which was still taking place on the Federal right; he saw the streams of disordered men who always hang about the rear of newly-raised armies, composed as both those were which contended at Shiloh. He saw the effects of the shells on these stragglers. He does not seem to have realized the importance of pushing the attack home, or the ease with which it could have been made. He failed to see that it was then a question of "now or never." It is clear that not 5,000 men, and those all more or less seriously shaken, were available to avert the final collapse of the Federal Army, had the Confederates pushed their victory home. Moments were all precious ; they were lost, never to be regained. It is impossible not to sympathize with the exclamation attributed to General Bragg : "My God ! Was a victory ever sufficiently complete ?" "My God ! My God! It is too late!"—*i. e.*, to carry out the attack because of the inopportune order to retreat.

General Beauregard's position during the earlier phases of the battle seems to have been more in accordance with the duties of a general in supreme command than were those rapid movements throughout the day, from point to point, of General Johnston. General Beauregard not unfairly observes, upon Johnston's frequent changes of position, that owing to them he was not able to govern the course of battle at all. As he puts it at page 588 :

"At no time does it appear from the reports of subordinates in any other part of the field that, either personally or by his staff, General Johnston gave any orders or concerned himself with the general movements of our forces. In fact, engrossed, as he soon became, with the operations of two or three brigades on the extreme right, it would have been out of his power to direct our general operations, especially as he set no machinery in motion with which to gather information of what was being done elsewhere or generally by the Confederate Army, in order to enable him to handle it intelligently from his position on the field."

It must be remembered that Johnston was the general in command until mortally wounded a little after 2 P.M. Beauregard, though probably better placed for directing the general operations up to that time, seems to have deprived himself of such staff as was left him, and not to have possessed sufficient authority, or sufficient means, to carry out the duties of command which Johnston had so largely vacated. Both Johnston and most of the headquarters staff seem to have been carried away by that longing, which all real soldiers experience, to be engaged in the close fighting line. It is a fatal mistake for a commander to give way to any such feeling, and a good deal of the incoherence in the execution of that day's well-conceived project—an incoherence which has been commented upon by almost all those who were present—seems to have been due to this. Indeed, there was so little unity of intention and direction throughout the day's operations that the absence of any one controlling spirit was apparent everywhere. Staff officers seem to have been going about issuing orders according to their own lights, without the smallest means of ascertaining what General Johnston's wishes actually were, without any clear knowledge of where he was, or even if he were alive,—and, as a matter of fact, he was not alive during part of the time I refer to. It was probably, on the whole, the less of two evils that orders should have been given even in this way than that troops should have remained out of action for lack of orders; but the chaos that must have necessarily ensued from all this is obvious. A committee directing a battle is an appalling condition of things to contemplate; but a dispersed committee, not even able to consult together, is a yet more certain cause of failure.

It would, therefore, be very unfair, in my judgment, to make General Beauregard, even after Johnston's death, responsible for the want of direction which is conspicuous in a good deal of this day's fighting. At the same time, it must be admitted that, when the Federals had been driven back, and the stress of battle had manifestly passed on towards the bank of the river, the time had come for the general in chief command to go forward. Had he done so, it does not seem that the battle would have ceased when it did. Had he then appeared upon the scene, the evidence goes to show that the reserve Federal artillery must then have been captured, and that, although the battle had been begun by the Confederates twenty-four hours later than it ought to have been, Buell would have arrived too late to save Grant's army from destruction. As has so often happened in war, the fight on either side was, it seems, considerably affected by the state of health of the two commanders. Had Beauregard been in his usual health, he would probably have ridden to the front between four and five o'clock in the afternoon. Had it not been for the severe fall, from the effects of which Grant was then suffering, probably there would not have been that absence of direction on the Federal side of which Buell speaks.

The numerous graphic sketches which are given of the "Hornet's Nest" are very interesting. The peculiar strength of the position seems to have depended on the fact that the assailants had to move out of cover across a rather narrow belt of open ground, against troops well posted under cover on the further side, the open space being also swept by flanking batteries. There is in the Niederwald, on the site of the battle of Woerth, a very similar clear break in the wood. The fire-arms of 1870 were, I suppose, a good deal more punishing than those of 1862. But this space was not flanked by any batteries; yet the whole German infantry of the XIth Corps were checked at this point, and unable to pass because of the conditions I have described. The analogy suggests some curious reflections as to the nature of ground that is most difficult for attacking troops to surmount.

As a student of war, I have endeavored to express, with impartial freedom, but, I hope, without offence to any one, these comments which the circumstances of this very interesting battle of Shiloh have suggested to me. Being in Canada at the time, I followed very closely all the newspaper accounts of it ; but its details have never been made so clear as by the accounts from many different quarters with which the *Century* Company have now supplied us. It would be impossible so to reconcile these different accounts as to satisfy all who took part in the action that justice had been done to the views which they advocate upon the responsibility of individual generals for failure and success. I think, however, that soldiers who desire to learn experience from these events will succeed in doing so much better by a perusal of the accounts given by the actors in this great drama, than from any ordinary pleasantly-sounded narrative. After all, it is as individual men, as actual soldiers, that we take our share of duty and responsibility, and the experiences of what other men have actually gone through are interesting, just because they represent the very partial view of a great action which we are, any of us, able to gain. We are able to see better how the swirl and whir of the battle surged round different parts of the field, by having laid before us the statements of what each actor saw and did in the performance of his own part.

I do not propose to touch, in any detail, the part that was played in these campaigns by the naval service on either side; but, for several reasons, very much interest attaches itself to the general scope and method of the combined land and water movements of this War. In the first place, owing to the many wars we have to carry on in wild and distant countries, the bearing of river transport upon military operations is a matter of great importance to our army. The subject is, therefore, especially interesting to us. Then, again, these full accounts of the methods pursued in these great river campaigns are of great value to English soldiers and sailors. Owing to our insular position, all operations of war, outside Great Britain, must necessarily begin with combined naval and military expeditions. It is, indeed,—according to Mr. Kinglake's happy phrase,—on our "amphibious strength" that we depend.

The magnificent sea-like rivers of the United States, and the essential dependence of the whole scheme of offence and defence, throughout this war in the West, on the retention or conquest of the course of the Tennessee, the Ohio, the Missouri, the Cumberland, and the Mississippi, make the whole character of the theatre of war and i · method of special interest to us. The originality and force with which all the resources and ingenuity of a great industrial and commercial people were thrown into the struggle, give to these combined naval and military movements a modern form, unique of its kind.

Each campaign is full of useful suggestions for us, upon the employment of similar means, should we, as seems more than likely, be forced to throw our whole strength into some—not in point of time—distant struggle for Imperial existence. There was, throughout all the phases of the detailed arrangements for this war, a similar originality in the adaptation of means to ends; as, for instance, in the Confederates' use of the bales of wet hemp during the siege of Lexington. I have preferred to deal first at large with these campaigns in the West, because the whole series hangs closely together, while the campaigns in Western Virginia and of the first Bull Run stand out like isolated combats, as far as this part of the history is concerned, and are much more closely connected with the history of the succeeding years. Indeed, as every one who writes of these campaigns in the West remarks, by the time that Donelson, Henry, Pea Ridge, Memphis, and Shiloh had been lost, the Confederate cause in the West was doomed. Vicksburg was more important as the final death-blow to that cause than as determining to which side victory should incline. The struggle for the great rivers was, during the earlier part of the War, almost as vital to the successful establishment of a Southern Confederacy as the defence of Richmond. When this period ended, the whole interest of the War shifted eastward and was concentrated on the line between Richmond and Washington.

Though, therefore, in point of date, the campaigns in Western Virginia and the battle of Bull Run preceded most of the events in Missouri and Tennessee, those campaigns are really the introduction to the history of the later period of the War. I may add that, except for the personal connection of General Beauregard with both Shiloh and Bull Run, and for the effect which was undoubtedly produced throughout the West by the Confederate success at Bull Run, the two series of events might almost as well have taken place on different continents, as far as any immediate influence which they exercised upon each other was concerned. The battle of Bull Run—certainly one of the battles of the war which have been most talked about and written about in Europe— would appear, from these accounts of it, to have gathered round itself, hitherto, a large margin of fiction and misconception.

As far as General Beauregard himself is concerned, there is a quaint historical parallelism between the battle of Shiloh and that of Bull Run. In neither was he the actual commander in point of seniority. In both, the actual commander seems to have left to him a certain authority on the battle-field, the nature of which has become the subject of subsequent fierce controversy. In the case of both battles, he succeeded in persuading the commander of forces engaged in a neighboring district to form a junction of both armies in his own district, with a view to crush one part of the enemy's forces, before that part which was in the neighboring district could be brought to its support. In both battles, the commander who so joined him was a General Johnston, though, so far as I am aware, there was not any family connection between General J. E. Johnston, who commanded at Bull Run, and Albert Sidney Johnston, who commanded at Shiloh; nor, to judge by the two likenesses on pages 228 and 542, was there the smallest personal resemblance between the two men. In both instances, the ground over which the battles were fought was much better known to General Beauregard than to either General Johnston. In both battles,—though here we enter upon more disputed ground,—the evidence seems clear that the general arrangements of the campaign had been thought out some time beforehand by General Beauregard, and that the other commander, on his arrival, almost inevitably accepted Beauregard's proposals. In both cases, the scheme of battle was so affected by unforeseen circumstances that at one, Shiloh, Beauregard himself, at the last moment, recommended the abandonment of the attack he had so ably planned, and at the other, Bull Run, where the enemy's forward movement left him no choice in that matter, his designed attack was converted into an almost purely defensive battle, carried out by a part only of the forces at his disposal. In both battles, taking account only of the first day's action at Shiloh, incidents occurred toward the end of the day which shook men's confidence in the man who had had the most share in the general planning of the campaign. In both battles, with whatever difference of cause and circumstance, those incidents were connected with a supposed too early stopping of the battle, and failure to drive the enemy to complete and final destruction. In both battles, General Beauregard attributed this early stopping of the action to the fatigue and exhaustion of his men, and to his want of food and ammunition for them. In both campaigns, he complained bitterly that he had not been supported properly by the civil authorities at Richmond. These analogies afford some food for reflection, and I leave readers to draw from them their own conclusions, which will probably differ not a little. The corrections which are supplied to the popularly-received account of Bull Run all seem to tend in the direction of substituting a picture of battle truly representative of what war really is for the kind of imaginative ideal of a battle which people at a distance love to create for themselves. General Beauregard says (page 216):

"It was a point made at the time, at the North, that, just as the Confederate troops were about to break and flee, the Federal troops anticipated them by doing so, being struck into this precipitation by the arrival on their flank of the Shenandoah forces marching from railroad trains halted en route with that aim—errors that have been repeated by a number of writers, and by an ambitious, but superficial, French author."

I am sorry to say that the error has been freely repeated by English as well as by French authors, and has even crept into some of our best-known text-books. The matter is of some importance, because it gives a false conception of the possible use of railways in war. It looks very pretty to draw a line of railway running at right angles to an enemy's line of advances, and to represent troops getting out of the trains and coming straight away from them to strike the exposed flank of the enemy. In the case of a pure infantry force, this might be possible, if it had been thought out beforehand. Very rarely indeed would it be possible for cavalry, and still more rarely for artillery. Moreover, where a mixed body of troops were coming by railway to an assigned railway junction, which, like Manassas, possessed some sidings and platforms provided for their disembarkation, it would very rarely be possible to disarrange the sequence of trains so as to disembark the infantry at some other point more important tactically, without disturbing the movement of the whole force, and probably causing much delay in the arrival of the troops upon the battle-field. Now, General Johnston, who actually directed upon the field at Bull Run the troops of Elzey and Early, which troops, in fact, turned the Federal right flank, tells us expressly (page 249) that Elzey, who arrived first with three infantry battalions, came from "Manassas Junction." Early, who came next, arrived with "Stuart's cavalry and Beckham's battery." The cavalry and artillery had evidently come up from Manassas, joining Early en route. It is clear that, essentially, this railway movement was purely one of general reënforcement. Manassas Junction lay far away to the right rear of that part of the Confederate line where the battle was actually fought. The overlapping of the Federal right was accomplished by movements made under General Johnston's own orders, advantage being taken of the concealment afforded by the woods near Chinn's house on the Federal right. Of the movements of General Smith, who at first commanded Elzey's brigade, Johnston says :

"He was instructed through a staff officer, sent forward to meet him, to form on the left of our line, his left thrown forward, and to attack the enemy in flank. At his request I joined him, directed his course, and gave him these instructions."

Moreover, the extreme troops on the Confederate left flank, and those which carried out the ultimate turning movement, were, so far as the infantry was concerned, not those which had arrived by railway at all, but Early's brigade, which had been in reserve behind Longstreet and Jones near Blackburn's and McLean's Ford, being, in fact, a part of Beauregard's own army. Thus it is as clear as possible that the important service which the Manassas Railway did for the Confederates was in putting them, strategically, in a military sense, as Beauregard says, "on interior lines" with regard to the two Federal armies of McDowell and Patterson. The really decisive fact of the campaign was the strategical transfer of Johnston's force from the Shenandoah region, unknown to Patterson. The turning of the Federal right was a tactical incident, due in part to the troops which were put at the disposal of the Confederate commander by that strategical transfer of force. In all essentials, the cause of the Confederate success was a movement like that which preceded the defeat of Hasdrubal by the Romans, or like that which preceded the battle of Blenheim. Almost all great military successes have these simple actions as their basis. Only, as has been said, it is that which is simple which in war is so very difficult.

Here, as in almost every other instance, the defeat of McDowell seems to have been due to the blunders of the authorities at Washington, acting under the influence of popular opinion. McDowell had fully foreseen the danger with which he was threatened. This is shown conclusively by his making it one of the conditions of his movement that General J. E. Johnston's force should be kept engaged by Major-General Patterson. Nothing can be clearer than this fact—that the Bull Run disaster, which so appalled public opinion in the North, was deliberately prepared for itself by that very public opinion taking upon itself to enforce its demands upon the generals in the field through the medium of its recognized exponents. General James Fry puts this well in separate paragraphs which are worth collating:

"General Scott, who controlled both McDowell and Patterson, assured McDowell that Johnson should not join Beauregard without having Patterson on his heels." (Page 181.) "Northern enthusiasm was unbounded. On to Richmond was the war-cry. Public sentiment was irresistible, and, in response to it, the army advanced." (Page 176.)

Yet, again, after showing how completely Johnston gave Patterson the slip, he says, "It rested, however, with higher authority than Patterson to establish between his army and McDowell's the relations the occasion called for" (note, page 183); and then he goes on to show how the public fear in the Capital of attack by the Shenandoah Valley obliged the Washington authorities to insist on Scott's not only keeping Patterson in the Shenandoah Valley, but actually reënforcing him at the moment when every man was required to reënforce McDowell. Furthermore, if Patterson was to keep Johnston from reënforcing McDowell, it could only be done by steady and persistent fighting. But he had been warned against fighting, lest the Capital should be exposed by want of "caution." *Hence*, as General Fry truly says, "as soon as McDowell advanced, Patterson was upon an exterior line and in a false military position."

To sum up, then, the indictment against the true criminal. Let us clearly understand that the prisoner at the bar is "Public Opinion." This is the case against him. He understood nothing whatever of military principles or the conditions of the movements of armies; yet he took into his ignorant hands the entire conduct of this part of the war. Without even realizing the connection between the several things which he required as a sacrifice to his imagined omniscience, he kept Patterson and all his forces in the Shenandoah Valley for fear lest Johnston should move on the Capital. Then, having deprived McDowell of all possible supports and crowded his camps with picnicking parties, "under no military restraint, that passed to and fro among the troops as they pleased," reducing indefinitely the fighting power of his army, the prisoner at the bar sent forward the unfortunate general and army to meet their fate from the two armies whose union he (the prisoner) had facilitated. Whom shall we hang? This thing, or the fine soldier whose portrait is given on page 170 ? Unfortunately, the number of convictions against the prisoner, and the freedom with which he secures the power to repeat his crimes, are so notorious that there is little use in convicting him. In 1861 he cries out madly, "To Richmond!" In 1870 his mad cry is, "To Berlin!" If only some one would make out a true record of all the crimes with which he has been justly charged, seeing that there is and can be no defence for him, one might hope that perhaps on some future occasion, some one or two of the host that go to swell his power, to tickle his vanity, and to lead his followers to destruction, might pause and consider. Even one or two strong men facing the stampede of an ignorant crowd that knows not where it is going, have often a wonderful power in breaking its force and in turning it aside from ruin. Therefore, it is worth while to seize such occasions as one may, to hold up to this creature, to this self-styled god, a mirror in which it may see its own likeness, and seeing it, and appalled by the image, may cower before perpetrating fresh crime. I doubt very much if the criminal is as powerful or as ignorant in the United States as he is among us. I believe, with Sir Henry Maine, that the creators of your Constitution showed their wisdom mainly in shackling his impatient hands; in at least providing for an appeal from him when he is drunk to the time when he is sober.

I can here only touch upon the first phase of the next fit of madness which, in 1861, seized him in the United States. I have always had a great respect for General McClellan. But to those who, having first caused the destruction of McDowell's army, carried out the next stage of the programme usual in such cases, namely, the discovery that McDowell was responsible for all they had done, and decided to replace him by a "Young Napoleon," the graphic details of the campaigns in Western Virginia, under McClellan's leadership, must be painful reading. If General Cox had tried to complete this part of my indictment against the reckless interference of Public Opinion in the conduct of military affairs, he could hardly have worded it more incisively than he has done, in what he himself describes as the "unvarnished tale" of the attack on Rich Mountain, and in his description of the mode in which it led to its one important consequence—the promotion of McClellan to the command of the Potomac Army. It would not be unfair to sum it up thus: McClellan arranged to detach a small turning force under Rosecrans to attack a flank of Rich Mountain. The success of such a movement ordinarily depends on the vigor with which other forces combine in the attack, and on the support afforded to the small turning force, which is otherwise dangerously risked. McClellan had undertaken to attack vigorously as soon as Rosecrans was heard to be in action. "The noise of the engagement had been heard in McClellan's camp, and he formed his troops to attack, but the long continuance of the cannonade, and some sign of exultation in Pegrans's camp, seem to have made him think that Rosecrans had been repulsed." Therefore, McClellan did nothing whatever; meantime Rosecrans, who had planned his own movement, and had volunteered for it, had, by extraordinary good fortune and good management, succeeded in carrying the whole position entirely with his own force. Thereupon the defence of the remainder of the Mountain collapsed. "On McClellan's part," beyond a rather timidly-conducted pursuit, "nothing further was attempted." McClellan, however, published a dispatch in which he congratulated his troops on having "annihilated two armies, commanded by educated and experienced soldiers, intrenched in mountain fortresses fortified at their leisure." "The country was," we are told, "eager for good news, and took it as literally true." Whereupon McClellan was photographed in the Napoleonic attitude, and duly promoted to the command of the Potomac Army, to be dealt with afterwards according to the time-honored fashion of that hoary-headed and cruel old rascal, Public Opinion, towards his broken idols.

WOLSELEY.

[TO BE CONTINUED.]

www.ingramcontent.com/pod-product-compliance
Lightning Source LLC
Chambersburg PA
CBHW032242080426
42735CB00008B/971